CHUCK CLOSE

FEBRUARY 25 - 26 MARCH 1983

THE PACE GALLERY 32 EAST 57 NYC 10022

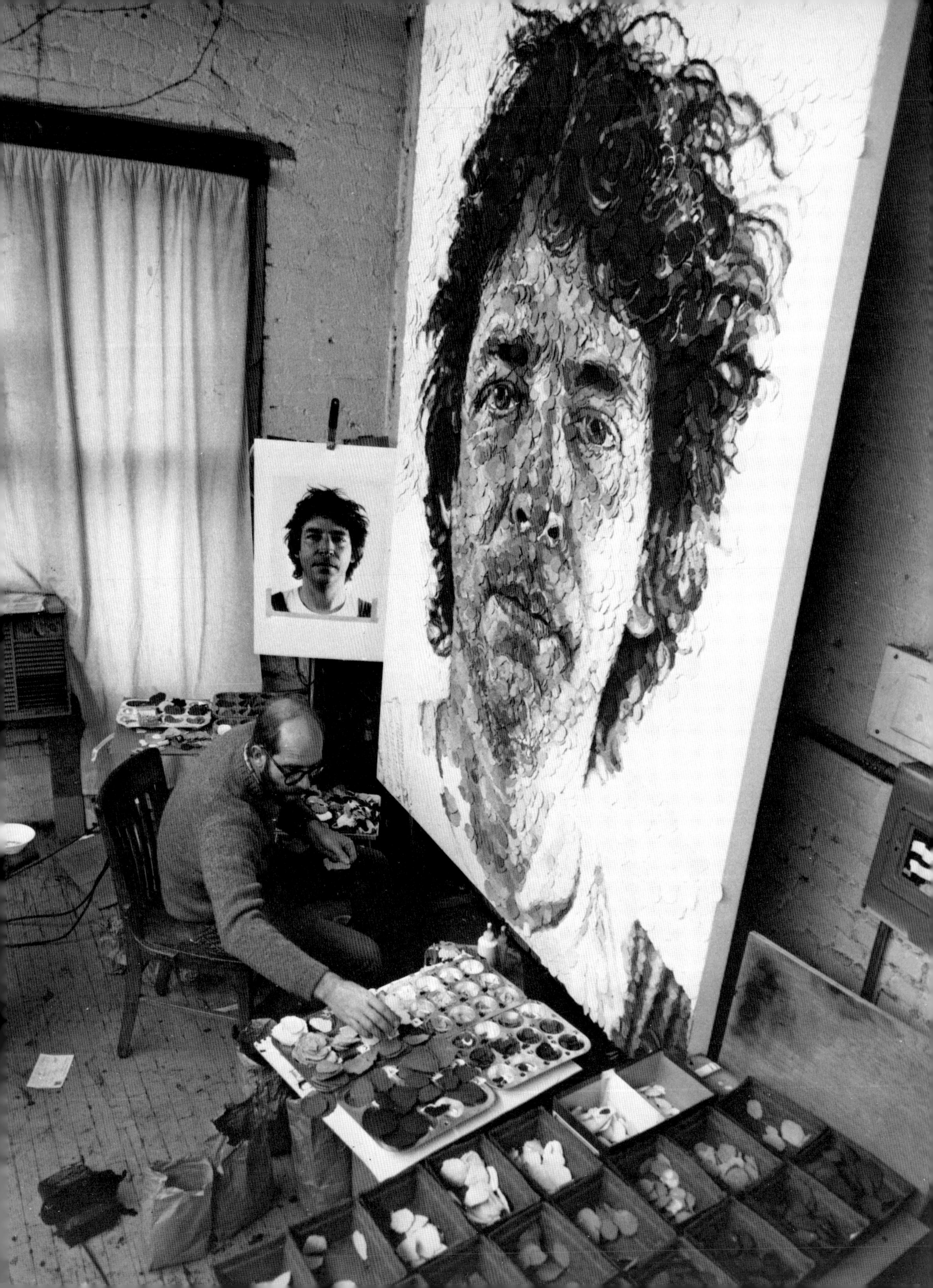

ON CHUCK CLOSE

John Perreault

A great deal is already known about Chuck Close's art. Countless solo and group exhibitions and a stream of articles, interviews, catalogue essays, and books on contemporary art have made his paintings and works on paper very well-known indeed. In 1980 and 1981 a retrospective of his art, initiated by the Walker Art Center in Minneapolis traveled to three other important art institutions: The St. Louis Art Museum, Chicago's Museum of Contemporary Art, and the Whitney Museum of American Art. The catalogue for the exhibition contains excellent essays by Martin Friedman and Lisa Lyons.[1] He has also exhibited internationally. The cumulative effect of all this well-deserved exposure is that no fair survey or discussion of contemporary art could exclude considerations of his art. Why is this so? The art itself has impact, at first acquaintance and, more importantly, after repeated viewings. Although firmly positioned within a network of contemporary art issues and approaches it is unique. It raises key questions.

We already know that more than a decade ago Close, through a series of art decisions rising from personal proclivities, studio practice, and problem solving, arrived at the basic parameters of his style, his field of activity. The vocabulary and the grammar of his pictorial/formal language may have seemed narrow at first, but self-imposed limits, particularly when they are as daring and intelligent as Close's, can generate freedom and depth as well as focus and consistency. Limits are not values in themselves. For every successful or moderately successful use of the principles of limitation there are innumerable failures. For every Josef Albers or Ad Reinhardt, for every Sol LeWitt or Chuck Close there are hordes of artists or would-be artists, convinced that self-imposed limitations are *the* art strategy (as if art could ever merely be a matter of strategy). Why waste good canvas, space, and time with trivial forms, images, or ideas? Limitations are to be judged by what they produce. Close's "limits"—severe enough to produce clarity, yet flexible enough to allow new challenges as he proceeded from one option to the next—have helped produce a remarkable body of work, notable for its intensity, conviction, and high-level of achievement.

Close's chosen subject is the human face or, more specifically, dead-pan, straight-forward (actually rather precisely engineered) photographs of the human face. His process of art-making is as important as the image and an equal part of the content of his work involves the painstaking transfer of the chosen image by hand through translation, transcription, and matching, using in turn in different works as he moves through the years: the air-brush, the brush, etching tools, pastels, his own fingers (in the fingerprint pieces), and in the current exhibition chips of handmade paper. In the continuous image works or paintings he has moved from the startling grissaille or black and white works to full-color paintings achieved by superimposing three monochromatic fields of image information derived from photographic color-separations. In the drawings, prints, and other discontinuous image works, where the grid is allowed to surface as part of the direct information, he has explored degrees of image resolution (and consequently image recognition) plus number, system, medium, density, texture, tactility, visible decision-making, error, and even gesture—suitably dispassionate and subdued, but gesture nonetheless. He has systematically investigated the grid as method and subject, as art sign and image field, but has not hesitated to substitute traced drawings of projected images as an alternative substructure, beginning with some of the fingerprint pieces and now in a good number of the paper-chip works.

All of this, save perhaps his move from the grid, which is a relatively recent effort, is known, as is his methodical use of studio time and, by contemporary standards, the enormous amount of work it takes him to complete his larger and sometimes even smaller pieces. Along with the aspects of his oeuvre already touched upon, his work is about work.

What then is not known, or if known, has not been said? Description and sometimes analysis of Close's art have been relatively accurate. Interpretations have been wavering as usual, but interpretations are always open to argument and revision. What has not been said is how it feels to see and be confronted by his art, what the experience is. Photos in magazines, catalogues, and books offer scant cues or clues, for, as handy as they may be, they cannot convey anything more than the basic information. We may read what the measurements are, but scale (which is always relative to rooms and bodies and other art works) can only be experienced directly. We may note the medium, but texture and physicality, like scale, must always be seen to be appreciated. Any attempt to convey the experience of an artwork through words, however, is usually open to the charge of subjectivity or, because it often involves metaphorical language, to the accusation that what one is doing is poetry or literature and not art criticism. This is as if art criticism—no matter how logical in its arguments or persuasive in its analysis, no matter how precise in its descriptive or interpretive detailing, no matter how fanciful or plain in its opinions or its tropes—could be anything else but literary. We do our best. And although we may circle the actual art experience, coming around to it again and again, as we will in the course of this essay, perhaps coming closer and closer to it, perhaps even ending with it as the final justification or basis of evaluation, we can never provide a substitute for it nor would we want to if we could. We do not duplicate; we point.

In the meantime, what has not been said—or at least not to my knowledge—and what can be said and defended quite clearly and directly is that Close is a major artist producing major art for well over a decade. In some respects he has been treated like a major artist: he is in the collections of major museums and there is already some literature on his work. These are significant signs, but there are lesser artists whose art biographies could match Close's almost point for point yet rare indeed would be the claims for major status. Perhaps there is a genuine reluctance in this day of hype and hyperbole to single out any artist as major; it might be construed as hype or hyperbole. Furthermore, depending upon one's philosophy, it might be seen as antidemocratic or in the service of maintaining other kinds of hierarchies, which, of course, is not necessarily the case. My feeling, however, is that no matter how sympathetic one may be to all artists, in the long run if one is to be faithful to the role of critic and therefore to art, value judgments cannot and should not be avoided. Some art is better than other art.

Contemporary art is in such turmoil that it is sometimes difficult to separate out the art that is truly worthy of more than passing attention. This takes experience, time and thought. So many styles and points of view compete for our awareness that they often seem to cancel each other out and reduce the possibility of serious judgment to matters of promotion, publicity or personal taste. Eventually, no matter what one's level of tolerance is or how broad one's tastes, it becomes clear that not all art is equal. Some art stays in the mind, is more puzzling or more beautiful, is more complex—no matter what its outward simplicity—and more disruptive or satisfying than other art. This art may be painting or sculpture; it may be abstract or representational; it may be emotional or intellectual or both. There are no rules, or it may be that the rules keep changing. Great art may be singled out after the fact, but it cannot be predicted—a circumstance that is the downfall of all academies and the bane of critics and curators.

At one point there seemed to be an opening and a need for a new figurative art, but instead of New Images of Man, as proposed by The Museum of Modern Art, we were taken off-guard by Pop Art. In opposition to and in response to Minimal Art, pleas for or predictions of a new emotional or expressionist art have so far yielded either mixed or rather superficial results. Presently one might hint that a new abstraction is due, yet fear that the results of such hints might forever haunt one's tentative and well-meaning hopes. Of course, all these kinds of art co-exist, if but in nascent form, and it is only the critical attention that changes. The system reinforces and through positive-feedback encourages what it wants by virtue of an informed consensus. This consensus takes continually surprising turns. Yet rising above this mechanism of taste and tastes, some art is major and most art is minor. Minor art, since it is usually not inept or totally off-base, could be called ordinary art, and ordinary art is pleasant to have around. The world would be a sadder, duller place without it, but it does not add anything to the art that already exists, to the theory of art, to perceptions of art or of the world.

What then is major art? There is no easy answer. Here the critic, like the artist, takes a risk, but hopefully a studied one. Many prefer to back away or avoid the issue, for it is within this arena that in time the judge will be judged. Neither felicity nor opacity of style, neither cleverness of argument nor richness of reference or rhetoric can shield the critic from the wrath or mirth of posterity. When you are wrong you are wrong forever. It is safer to leave the judgment of the art of our contemporaries to some future consensus. Important art is art that withstands the test of time. But for how many generations must we wait, for how many swings of the pendulums of taste? Surely there is more to art than being able to brave the vicissitudes of fashion. Besides, fashion never sleeps. The future might be wrong. Surely there is something about major art that is *present* and therefore timeless, no matter how much a product of a particular time and place. Posterity? What is forgotten, perhaps with purpose, is that we ourselves create posterity. What we say and do now influences what will be said and done next, even and most particularly if the next word or deed is a contradiction of what we have been saying and doing. We are not entirely working in the dark. We have become finely tuned art-machines.

Nevertheless, one traditional definition of major art is that it is art that lasts, but there is no reason to be limited to this future condition. We have some inklings of the characteristics of art that might last. We mean, I suppose, art that will last, not only physically—there are storerooms for that—but spiritually. It will continue to offer an esthetic experience beyond the moment. It will be worth looking at and thinking about next year and the year after that until the art in question is inseparable from art history and culture. The quality of probable lastingness is what we mean by quality. On some level the question can only be answered by working from an understanding of those qualities that in the past have contributed to lastingness, that still operate in the present, and that are likely to continue to operate in the future. Beyond a certain level of skill and clarity of presentation, these qualities are deflection, reflection, ambition, timing, positioning, innovation, and uniqueness of statement. Chuck Close's art exhibits all of these qualities.

Of these qualities deflection is likely to be the most unfamiliar and difficult, though once grasped the concept of deflection is illuminating and might even be seen to underlie most other characteristics of major art. It has the virtue and the drawback of picturing the course of art rather abstractly in terms of problem-solving and system, but if handled correctly it need not be reductive. Deflection does however take away some of the romantic heroicism of art-making by locating invention and innovation in a larger and perhaps less personal realm of creativity, tending to balance conception with notions of reception, thus reconceptualizing the course of art as discourse rather than as the descent, progress or evolution of art.

As far as I know, it was Henry Geldzahler who first used the terms "deflection" and "deflector." Under the influence of George Kubler,[2] whom he quotes, in 1969 Geldzahler wrote the following in an introductory catalogue essay: "As curator, my guiding principles in deciding which artists to include in the exhibition 'New York Painting and Sculpture: 1940-1970' have been the extent to which their work has commanded critical attention or significantly deflected the course of recent art. These 'deflectors,' as they may be called, are those artists who have been crucial in redirecting the history of painting and sculpture in the past three decades."[3]

The exhibition itself, although mildly controversial at the time (only one out of the 43 "deflectors" was a woman, which may have been chalked off to description if some of Geldzahler's other selections had not been perceived of as doubtful or arbitrary) is now virtually forgotten. Nevertheless, Geldzahler's deflection concept remains useful. It could present art as a dialectic, with equal weight given to past, present, and future, as opposed to art as the fulfillment of supposed stylistic determinents arranged in a tradition or art as denial of tradition. The course of art is still seen as a stream (as in the term "mainstream") but this course is not inevitable and predetermined, but instead a zigzag of obstacles and changes over a human terrain, balancing out personal initiatives and cultural contexts within time.

Deflection, however, should not be simplified into the notion of direct influence upon subsequent artists in terms of style or technique. Deflection may be a closing off as well as an opening up. The course of art, in this expanded and more accurate formulation, consists not only of artist-to-artist influences via artworks, but also of what might be called the critical discourse. This includes artist-to-artist communications via verbalizations of concepts, artist-to-critic, and artist-to-critic-to-artist transmissions. It even includes critic-to-artist and critic-to-critic interpretations, formulations, descriptions, and exhortations.

Keeping in mind the enriched meaning of the term, is Chuck Close a deflector? The answer is in the affirmative. If one were to propose an exhibition that would single out the most important art of the last fifteen years, Close would have to be included. It is not that he has inspired a wealth of imitators. So powerful is Close's art statement that only minor artists would dare to produce variations of his work. Variations such as the gridded still-life or landscape would only be trivial. Though the single-minded plainness of his no-nonsense approach to art-making may have influenced artists working in other areas—just as he was probably influenced by Albers and Reinhardt—the formal/pictorial level of his work acts as deflection by virtue of closure. Obstacle like, his art now deflects the art possibilities to other areas. Albers "owns" the square-within-a-square color exercise, Reinhardt the five foot cruciform in shades of black. Close owns the photo-derived, deadpan face with all the variations he can manage. More importantly, his work is unique in its positioning, offering a full-fledged and unarguable synthesis of minimalist, conceptualist, and process art concerns with unapologetic image-making or representation. This synthesis offers an opening that enlarges the art discourse.

After Close, no serious and fair analysis of contemporary art can ignore the recognizable image or dismiss figurative art prima facie as non-modernist and beyond the pale. One might argue that Pop Art had already accomplished this legerdemain, but Pop, for all its charm, wit, and real achievement, still has overtones of art as entertainment, a quality that continues to mitigate so-called high seriousness. Although the works of Close employ the representational image—

sometimes to such a high degree of verisimilitude that the coding, unlike in Pop, is initially transparent—like the works of the pure abstractionist (e.g. Malevich, Mondrian, Pollock, or LeWitt) the results are devoid of irony. In relationship to a great deal of post-Pop representational art, Close's work is also devoid of nostalgia and sentiment, two additional qualities that work against high seriousness.

Close's positioning within the art spectrum reflects and addresses issues of contemporary realism *and* issues of system and process, the latter usually only associated with non-representational art. His entrance—although it is hard to say

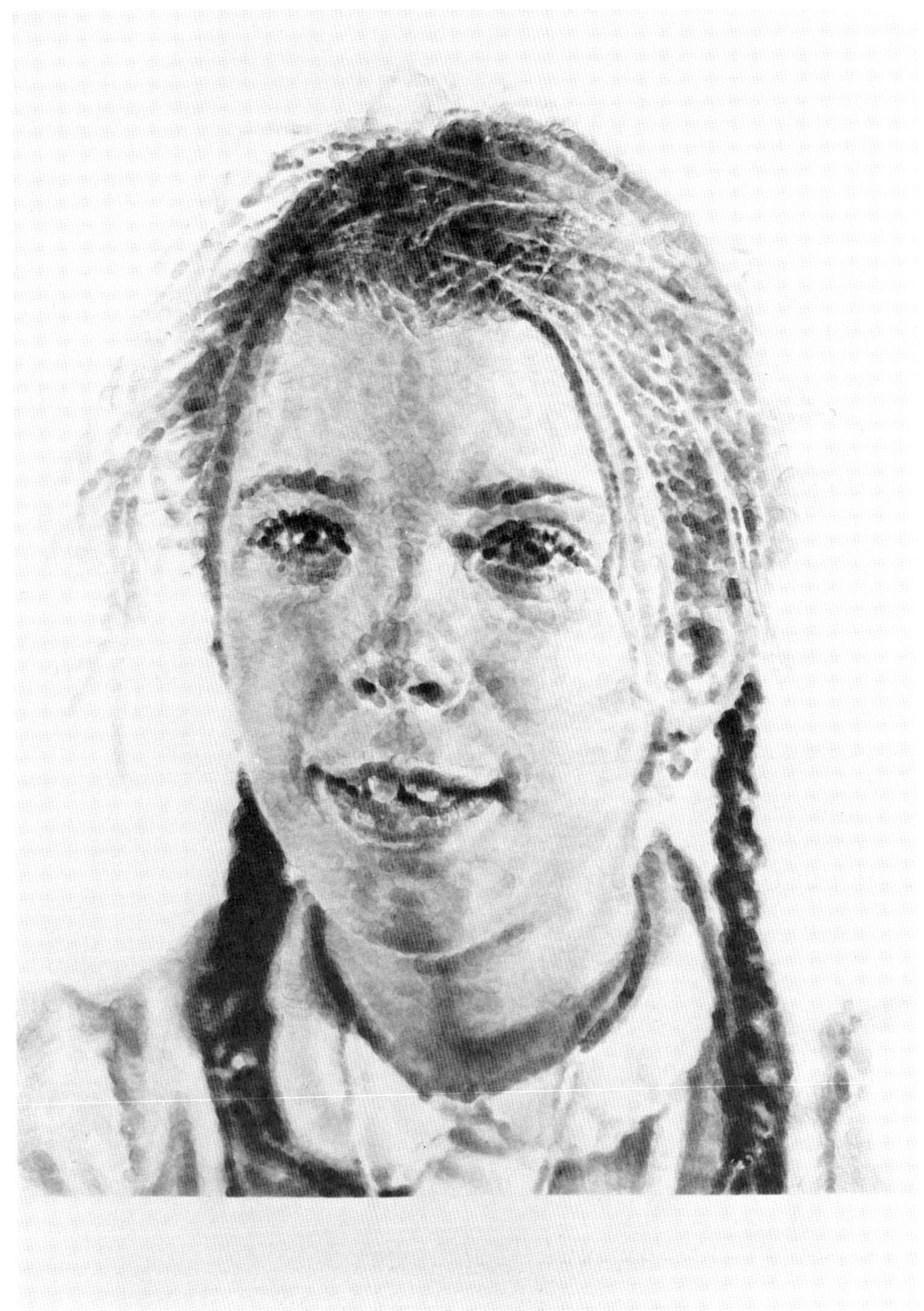

Georgia, 1980, fingerprint (stamp pad ink) on paper, 43 x 30½″

when and if an artist has control over this—was perfectly timed: by the late sixties Pop had already paved the way for a less ironic and less mass-media oriented figurative art, as had the work of the directly-from-life realists such as Philip Pearlstein, Alex Katz, and Alfred Leslie, among others. Minimalist, conceptualist, and process ways of making art were also well on their way to becoming firmly established, at least within the critical discourse. Close stepped in to be the one artist to combine both of these tendencies, while also being received as one of the first of the Photo-Realists.

Although a filling in of the grid (as in minimalist grid painting) in retrospect seems inevitable, Close's use of figurative information to do this was totally unexpected yet was positively received by at least some of the minimalists as a logical and a successful extension of systemic, minimalist and possibly even conceptualist principles. Nevertheless, Close has never considered himself a minimalist or a conceptualist. He was also generally perceived as a realist of the new subspecies called Photo-Realism. This was at first disconcerting to him, since he saw little connection between his work and other artists in this rather new category of Photo-Realism. As Duchamp once indicated there is usually a gap between intentions and results, which he called the art coefficient, and therein is the rawness and by implication the important aspect of art which may later be completed by the reception of the art.[4] The plain fact is that whether Close intended it or not, he is both a minimalist/conceptualist *and* a realist. Even the most intellectual art is open to interpretations and the possibility of unintentional meanings that escape the artist's control.

Looking at a Chuck Close work it would be impossible to see it completely outside the context of Photo-Realism. The image is always of a human face. In the case of the continuous tone works in particular, it is clear that the work is based on a photograph. Some works minutely duplicate the photo-chemical sign system, with all its vagaries of perspective and modeling, to such a degree that the uninformed might mistake the painting at first for a photo blow-up. Even in the broken-tone drawings, etchings, and now the paper-chip works, where the grid or process of matching is in the foreground and more overtly part of the immediate subject matter, enough signs remain to indicate a photo-source. There is, of course, a hidden history of the use of photography in art. Artists as varied as Delacroix, Eakins, Gauguin, Degas, and Picasso are now known to have used photographs upon occasion. Prior to the invention of photography other kinds of optical tools were in use.[5] What is different about Photo-Realism is that the photo source is not disguised. It is used without apology; in some respects it is celebrated. In some of the best examples of Photo-Realism the photograph and the photo-mechanical system of representation is a major aspect of the content of the art. This is the case with Close.

We know that Close's use of representational images, no matter how particulated or deconstructed they may become, is what distinguishes his work from other artists utilizing the grid, all-over composition/noncomposition, system, single-image frontality. But how is his work distinguished from other examples of Photo-Realism? Much Photo-Realism may be seen as Post-Pop Realism[6] or a direct off-shoot of Pop: Malcolm Morley's early and remarkable paintings of images from steamship brochures are the best and purest examples, but this aspect can also be seen in the work of the car-culture painters. Tones of irony, nostalgia and sometimes sentiment prevail. As already indicated Close's works have none of these qualities. Although strictly speaking it may be a matter of degree, Close's work most clearly appropriates the photo as subject, and in this regard he stands head and shoulders over the other Photo-Realists. Not only does he eschew irony, nostalgia and sentiment, he avoids narrative and allegory. There is nothing wrong or innately anti-esthetic about narrative and allegory—and possibly not even about irony, nostalgia, and sentiment—but Close is truly the purist of the Photo-Realists. That this change of degree makes a change of kind may eventually be seen.

Several kinds of defenses can be made for Photo-Realism, and in as much as Close is a Photo-Realist most of these apply to his work too. An argument by precedent has already been indicated by citing a number of artists in the past who have used the photograph. If one believes that art should reflect contemporary life, it is possible to see photo-painting as a direct response and perhaps comment upon the ubiquity of photography, from snapshots to billboards. But there is also a formal argument. Since Close as a Photo-Realist is the most formal artist within this category, this argument, though it may relate his work to some aspects of Pop, is singularly appropriate.

Starting with the prestigious but suspect premise that each form of art must seek, affirm, and in some sense limit itself to its own unique and defining properties, a case has been made that painting, for instance, should not be narrative, theatrical, or literary. Above all it should not appropriate more than two dimensions, even by the use of illusion, since the three dimensions are the realm of sculpture. Painting should be flat. That this flatness can only be achieved by an undifferentiated surface, since any mark will illusionistically "carve" into the surface, and that when flatness is achieved it emphasizes the objectness and therefore the sculptural relief qualities of a painting, need not be gone into here. It is enough to have a general outline of this most influential of art theories.

If one accepts flatness as a goal for high art painting, but also wishes to utilize or factor back into the art equation some degree of representation, for whatever personal or cultural reason, how might that be accomplished? The solution seems to have been to make representational paintings of things in the world that are generally perceived of as flat. Hence we have Jasper Johns' flags, targets and maps, followed by the cartoon frames of Roy Lichtenstein and the newsprint photos of Andy Warhol and so forth. If newsprint photos, why not less mediated images or photos themselves? Thus Chuck Close, whose works among all the Photo-Realists are the most nakedly photo-oriented, becomes a formalist of considerable import. Paradoxically, the new paper-chip works build out from the surface.

At this point it should be clear that Close's work has the qualities of deflection, reflection, timing, and positioning. But what of the three remaining qualities of major art? These are ambition, innovation, and uniqueness. Ambition does not mean careerism, but instead a will towards public statement and a willingness to address difficult art issues and to compete directly with the art of the past. Although he may use his friends and family as photo-subjects out of convenience and familiarity, Close's giant portraits and even the not-so-giant works take the form of public address. The scale of individual works and the scale of his entire systematic undertaking indicate that he is working towards the definitive, if not the universal. Through his day to day work—there is something most quotidian about his process of art-making—he is creating an oeuvre that in its consistency and variety clearly claims to stand up to the major art achievements of the past.

Close is also an innovator; he is not producing novelties, which are for amusement's sake and usually only of momentary value. Instead he has genuinely expanded some notions about what can or cannot be serious art. His art is also unique, for although it shares some characteristics with other Photo-Realists and with other minimalists it cannot be confused with the work of any other artist. Futhermore this uniqueness is meaningful.

Thus it is that on some level it may be proved that Chuck Close is a major artist producing major work. But have we been too rational, too logical? Could not any number of lesser artists be similarly justified by a similar chain of arguments and assertions? I think not. What then of the actual experience of the art? Is not that the final proof?

We cannot separate the art experience from the art context of information which includes all the factors already suggested and more. There is no naked eye. Nevertheless, the art experience no matter how tied to time, temperament, and taste is indeed of central importance. The art experience, however, can only be shared indirectly. To some extent throughout the above this may already have been done. To pursue the matter further one must shift to another mode of critical discourse: to the personal, the intuitive, and perhaps the poetic. Towards that end I can attempt to report how it has felt to look at Chuck Close's art over the past thirteen years.

From the very beginning, the work was disconcerting and somewhat disorienting, yet the shock of the enlarged photo-images soon wore off and I was able to see that although the work was monumental it was in no way dehumanizing; though it was cool, it was not cold. As the work unfolded in exhibition following exhibition, what at first was only my intuition, was proved: here was an extraordinary and engaging artistic intelligence at work. I personally put a high premium on the quality of intelligence in art and upon clarity too. I do not see clarity and even a certain plainness and stubborness as opposed to complexity, but rather as the usual preconditions.

From another point of view, the work is an assault, for we can all identify with the human face, particularly the ordinary human face—which may be why Close has never painted celebrities or political figures. But the faces are so large or sometimes so decomposed into squares or, as currently, chips of gray paper, that you are drawn closer and closer to them until they become landscapes or a series of almost autobiographical marks and decisions. They become maps of the artist's working process, which we can then identify with on a very human level. One imagines how it must feel to work at these, bit by bit. There is something very down-to-earth involved that celebrates work and commitment. And because Close avoids psychology in his portraits (they are indeed portraits, but perhaps of a new sort) the respect for personhood and privacy communicates dignity. From time to time Close alters his working procedure and his medium, but these qualities have endured.

The new work, a series using chips of variously tinted handmade paper to create new and familiar faces, shows an increased interest in texture and a looser presentation of process. This adds significantly to his art without losing one iota of the ground already covered. When one looks at a Close artwork a special awareness is likely to happen: many levels of perception and conception are quickened and engaged: a calm poetic steals through theorums of image and plane. This presently is as close as I can come to communicating *my* experiences looking at Close's art. The directness of the art sticks in the mind with the force and the mystery of a perfect metaphor. The literal transcends itself in a completely nondiscursive way.

[1] Lisa Lyons and Martin Friedman, *Close Portraits* (Minneapolis: Walker Art Center, 1980).

[2] George Kubler, *The Shape of Time* (New Haven: Yale University Press, 1962).

[3] Henry Geldzahler, *New York Painting and Sculpture: 1940-1970* (New York City: E.P. Dutton, 1969), 23.

[4] Marcel Duchamp, "The Creative Act" in *The New Art* ed. Gregory Battcock (New York City: E.P. Dutton, 1966).

[5] See: Van Deren Coke, *The Painter and the Photograph* (Albuquerque: University of New Mexico Press, 1972).

[6] See: Lawrence Alloway, "Art As Likeness (with a Note on Post-Pop Art)" in *Topics in American Art* (New York City: W.W. Norton, 1975).

Upper left: **Frank**, 1980, fingerprint (stamp pad ink) on paper, 15¾ x 11½"
Upper right: **Keith**, 1980, fingerprint (stamp pad ink) on paper, 15¾ x 11½"
Lower left: **Robert**, 1980, fingerprint (stamp pad ink) on paper, 15¾ x 11½"
Lower right: **Phil**, 1980, fingerprint (stamp pad ink) on paper, 15¾ x 11½"

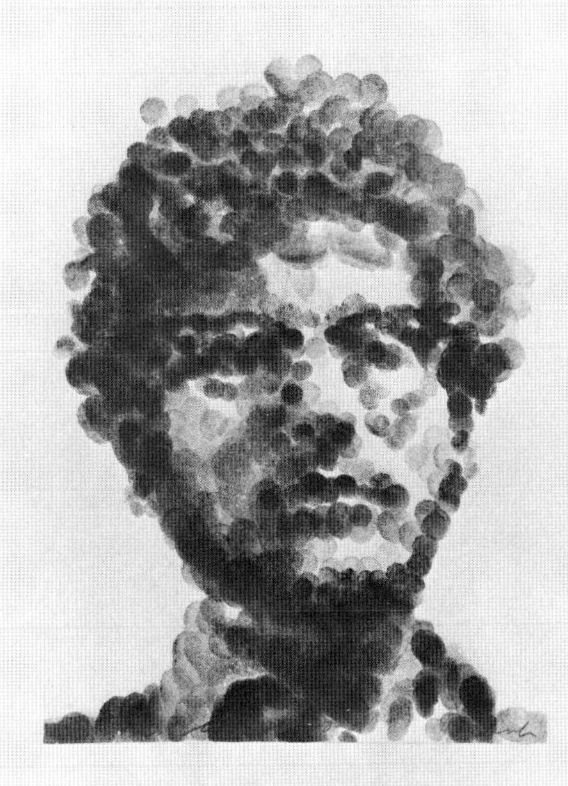
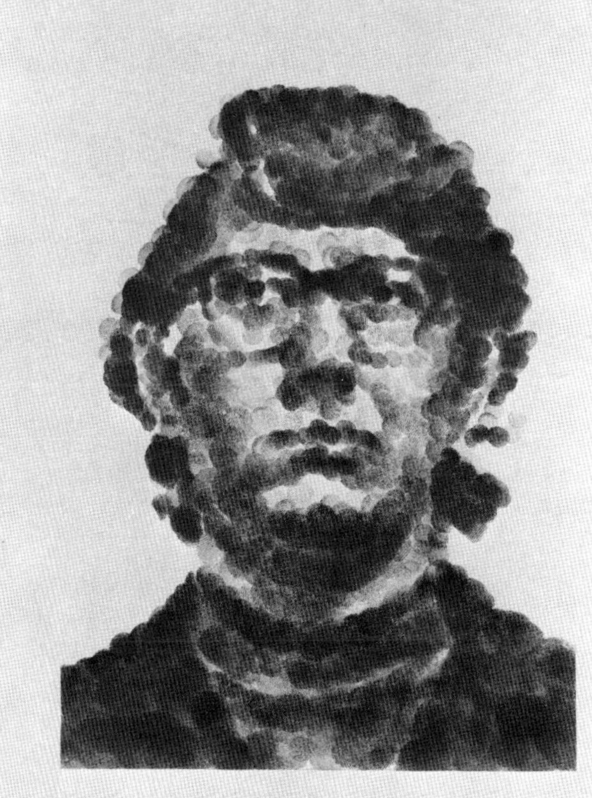
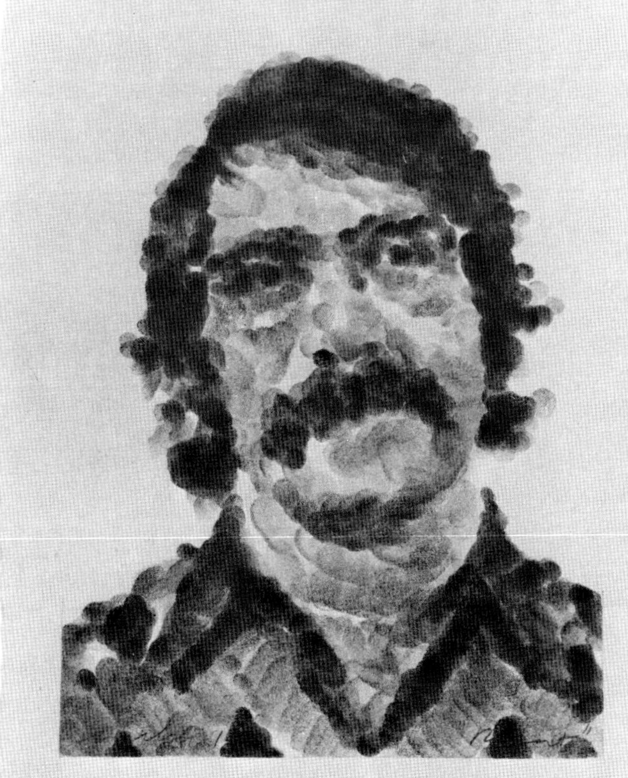
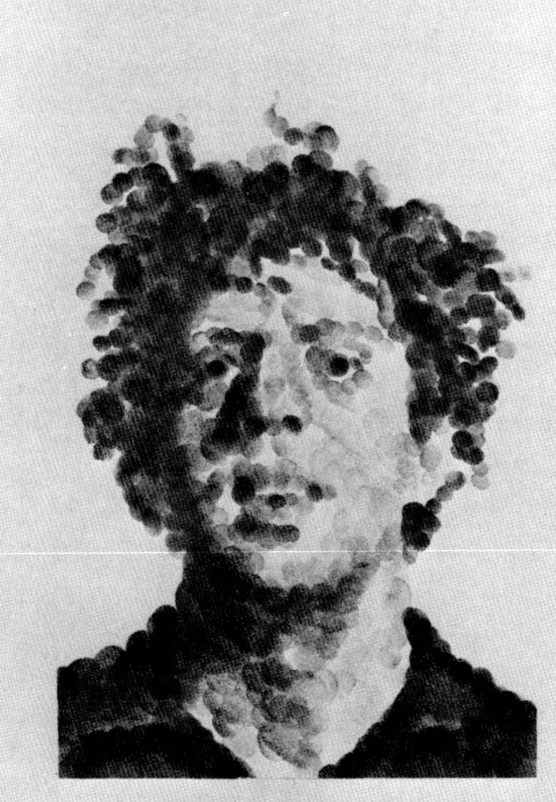

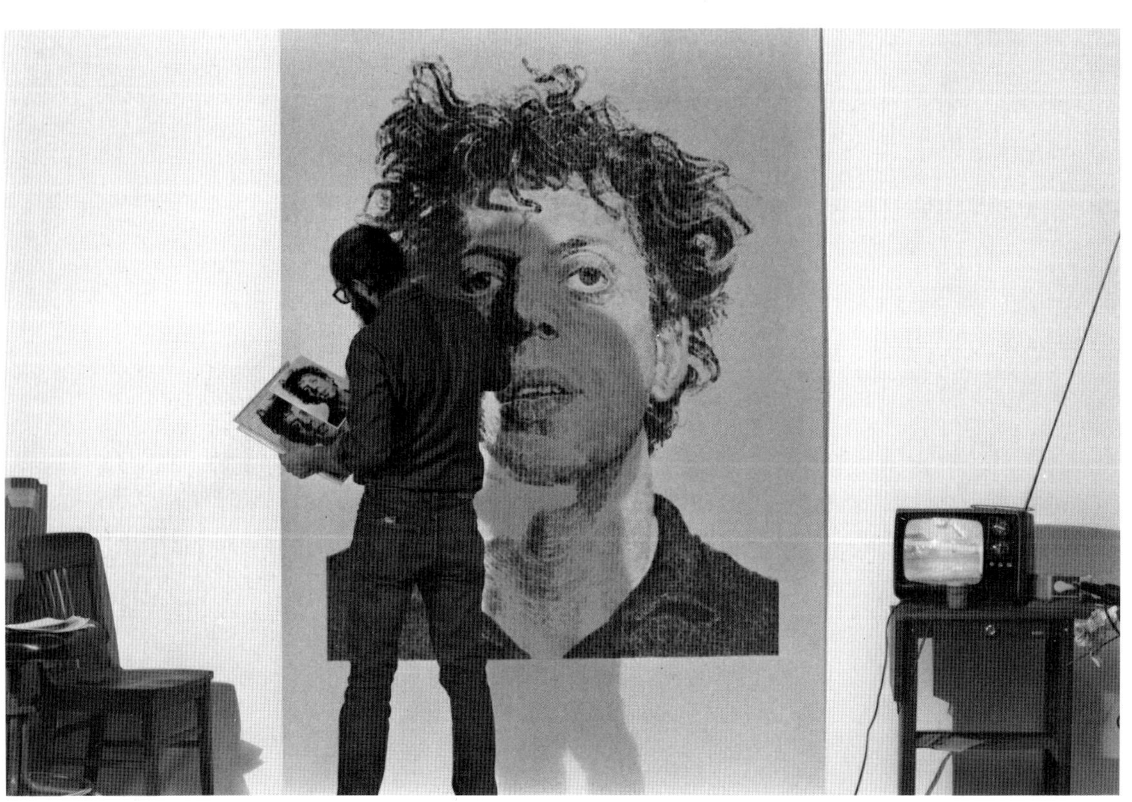

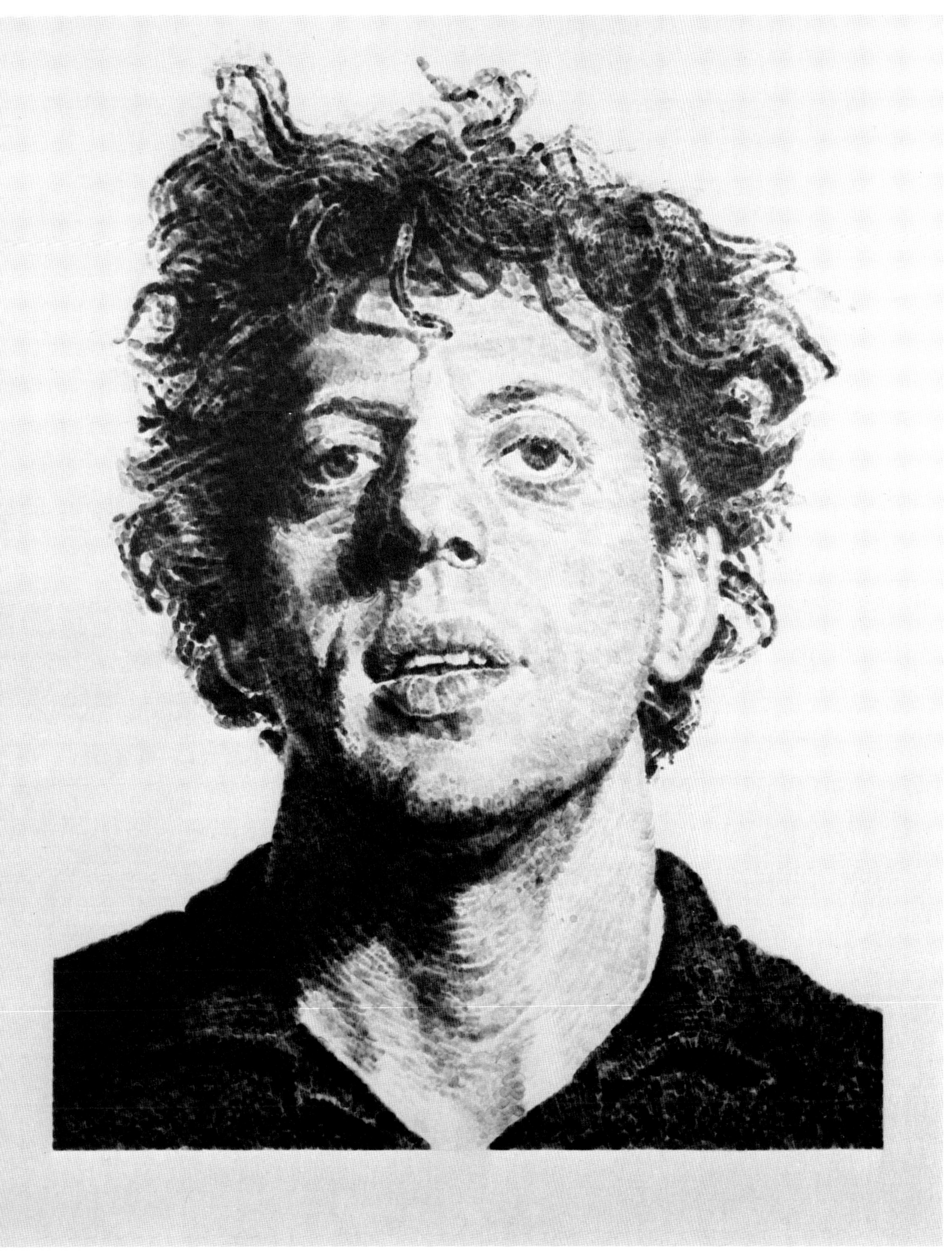

Phil/Fingerprint, 1980, fingerprint (stamp pad ink) on paper, 93 x 69″

Dick, 1981, fingerprint (stamp pad ink) on paper, 43¼ x 30¼"

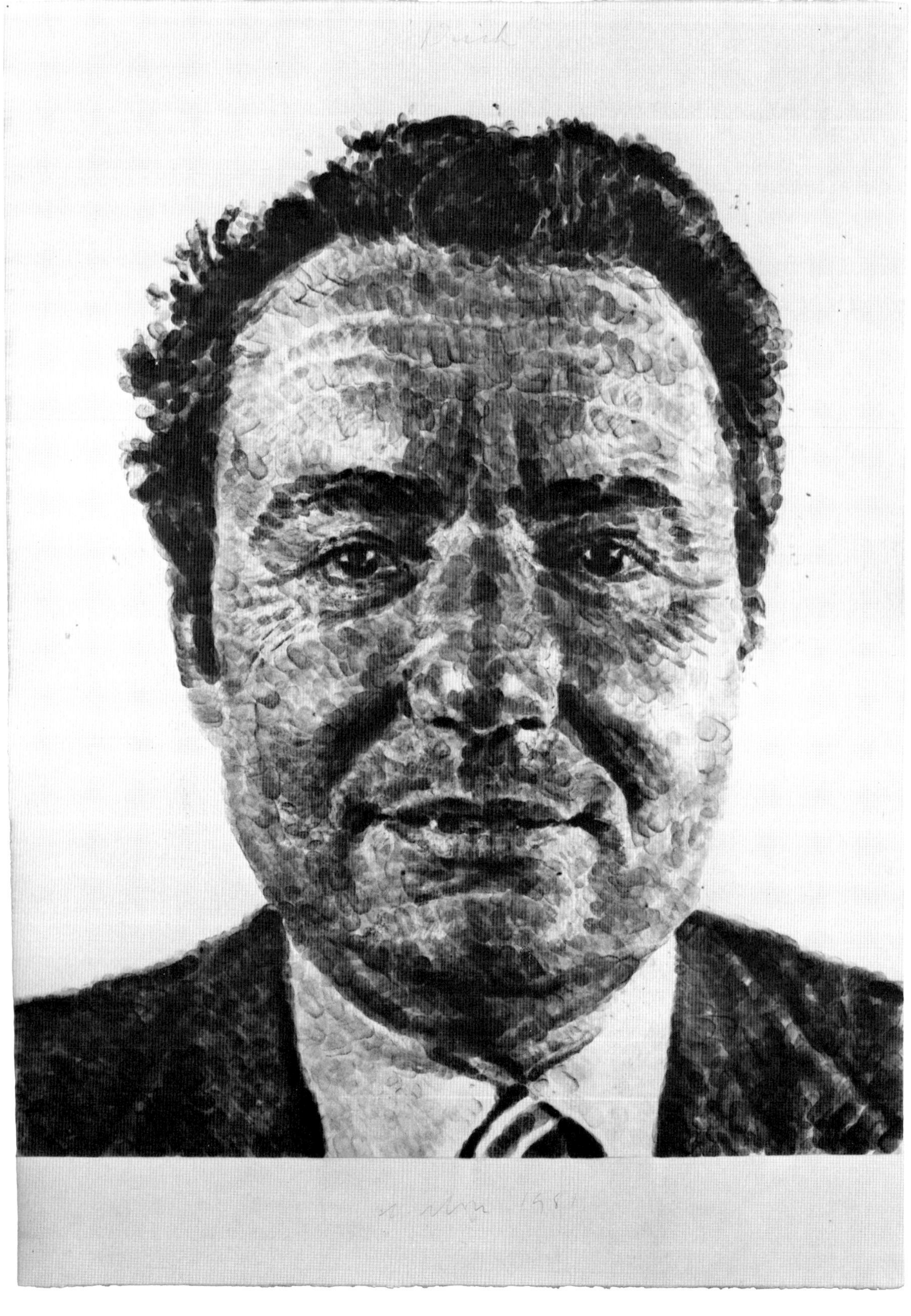

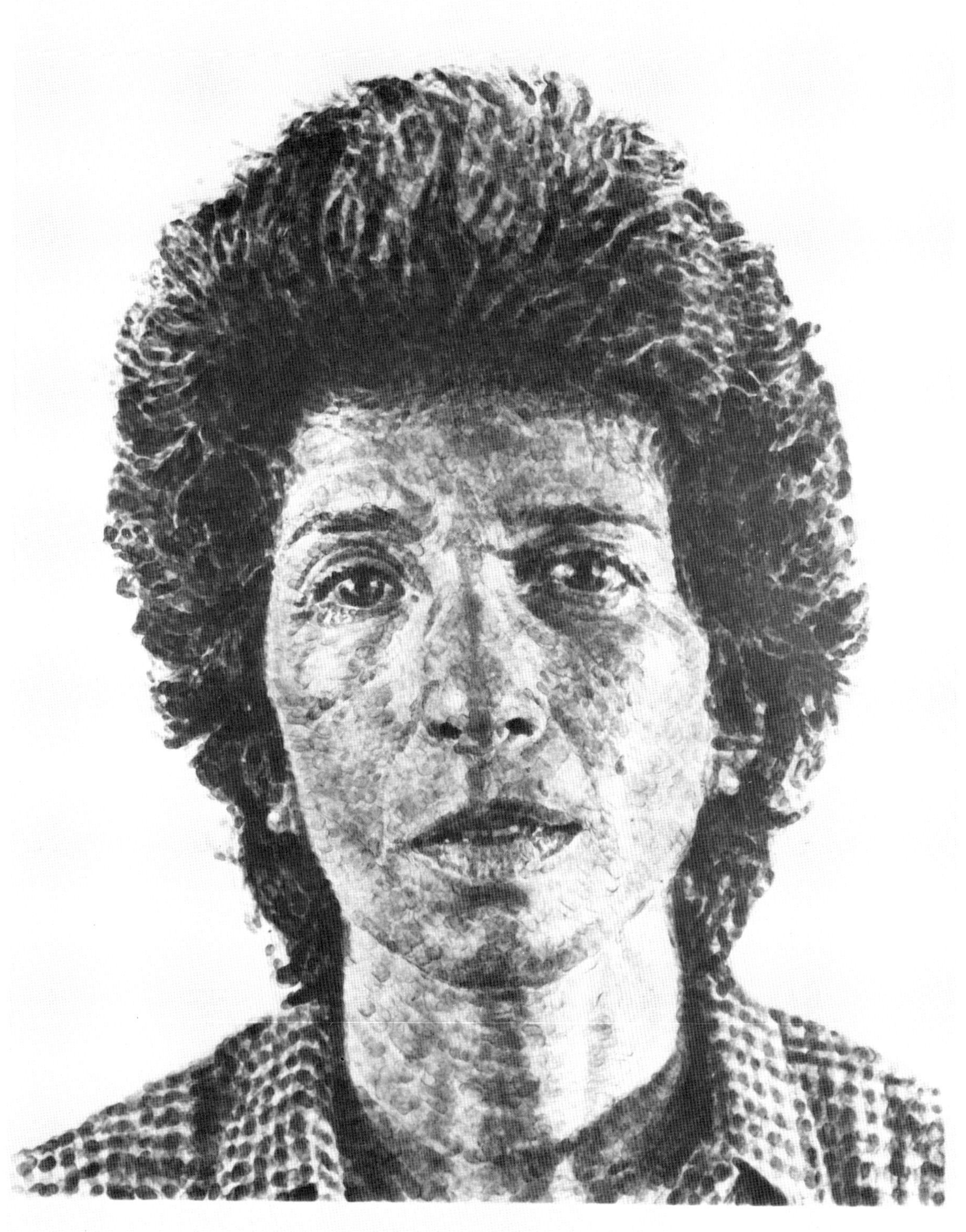

Phyllis, 1981, fingerprint (litho-ink) on paper, 57½ x 40¼″

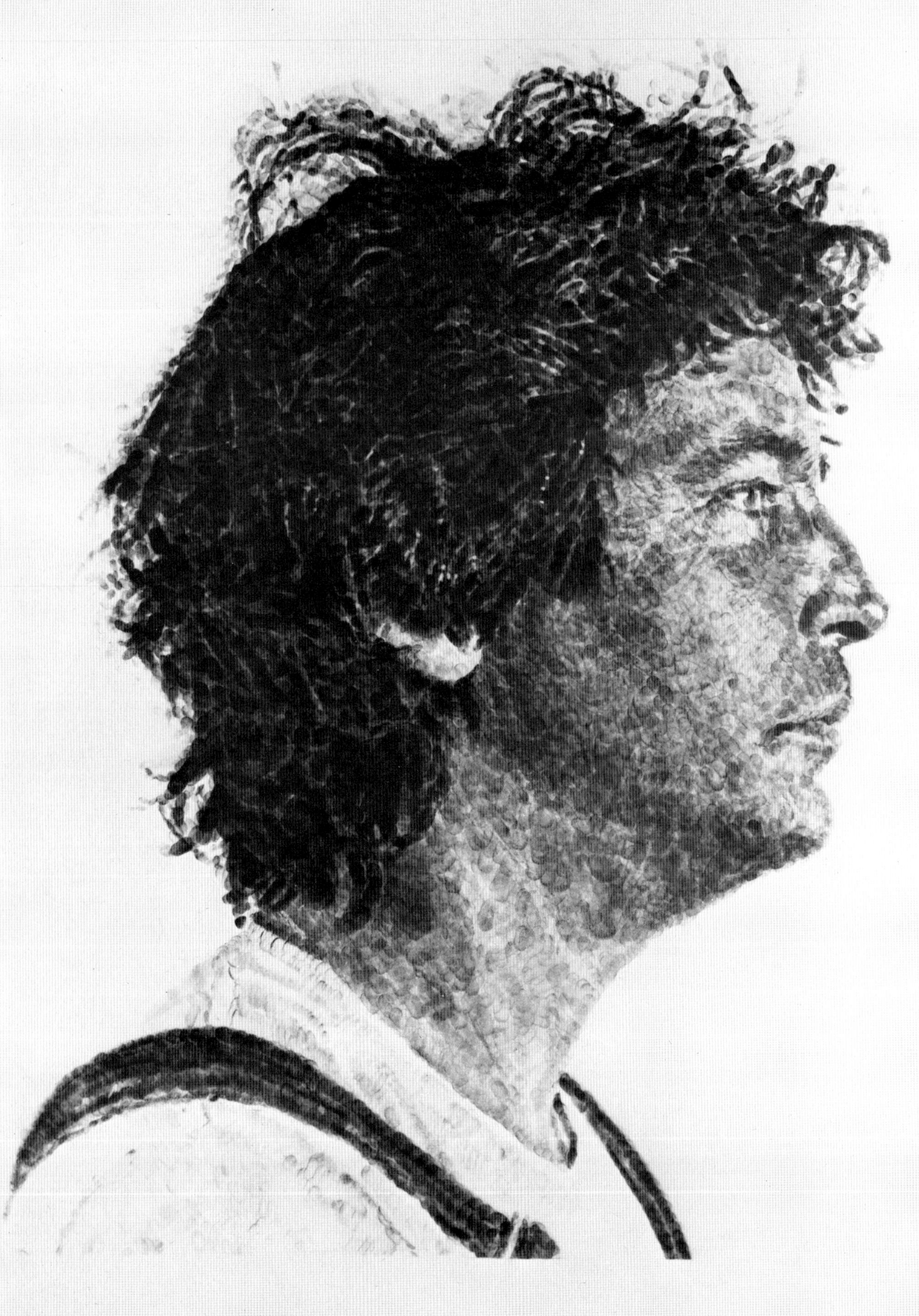

Jud,1981, fingerprint (litho-ink) on paper, 57½ x 40″

Arne (second version), 1981, fingerprint (litho-ink) on paper, 43 x 30½″

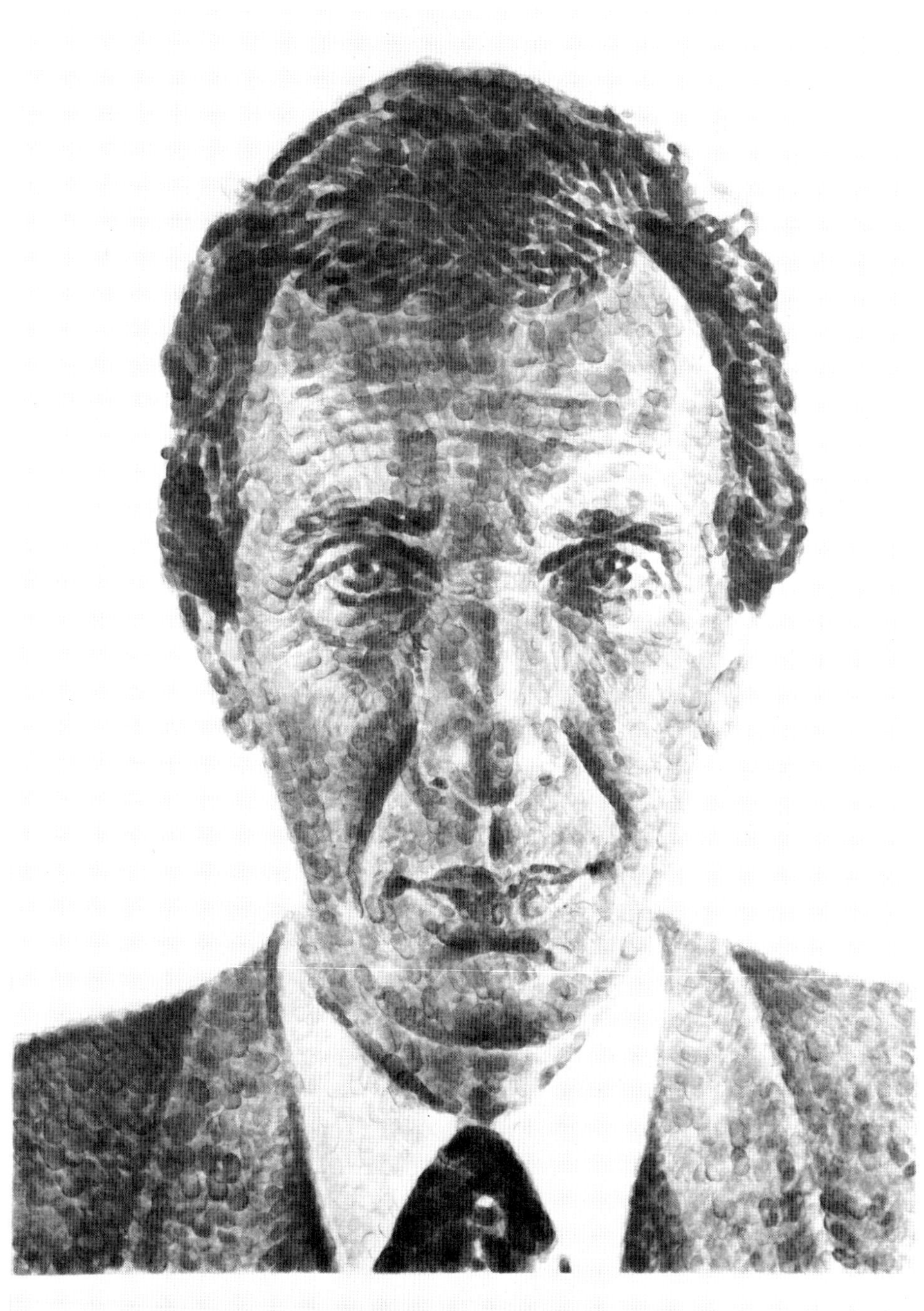

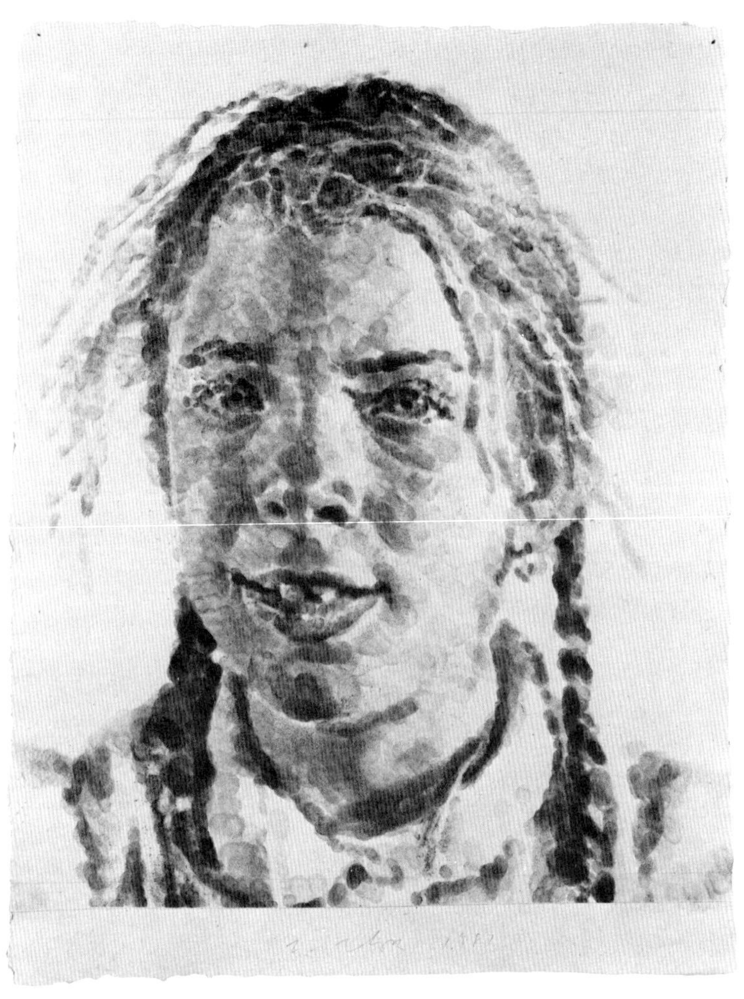

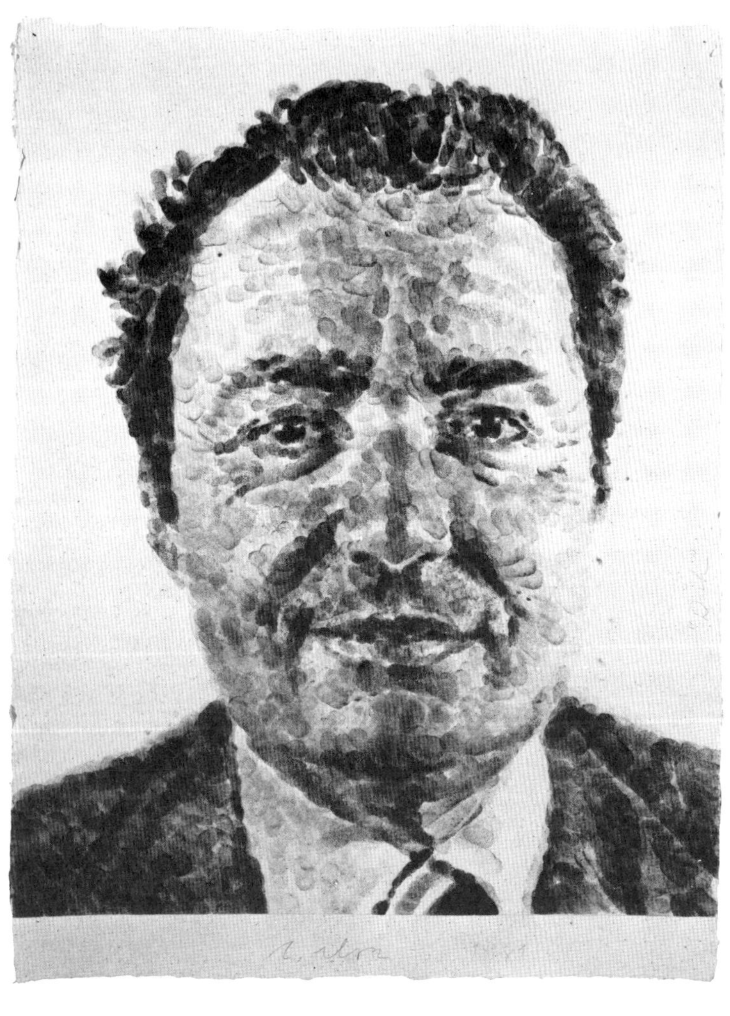

Georgia, 1981, fingerprint (stamp pad ink) on paper, 29 x 22″

Dick, 1981, fingerprint (stamp pad ink) on paper, 29 x 21¾″

Frank, 1980, fingerprint (stamp pad ink) on paper, 42¾ x 30¼″ ▷

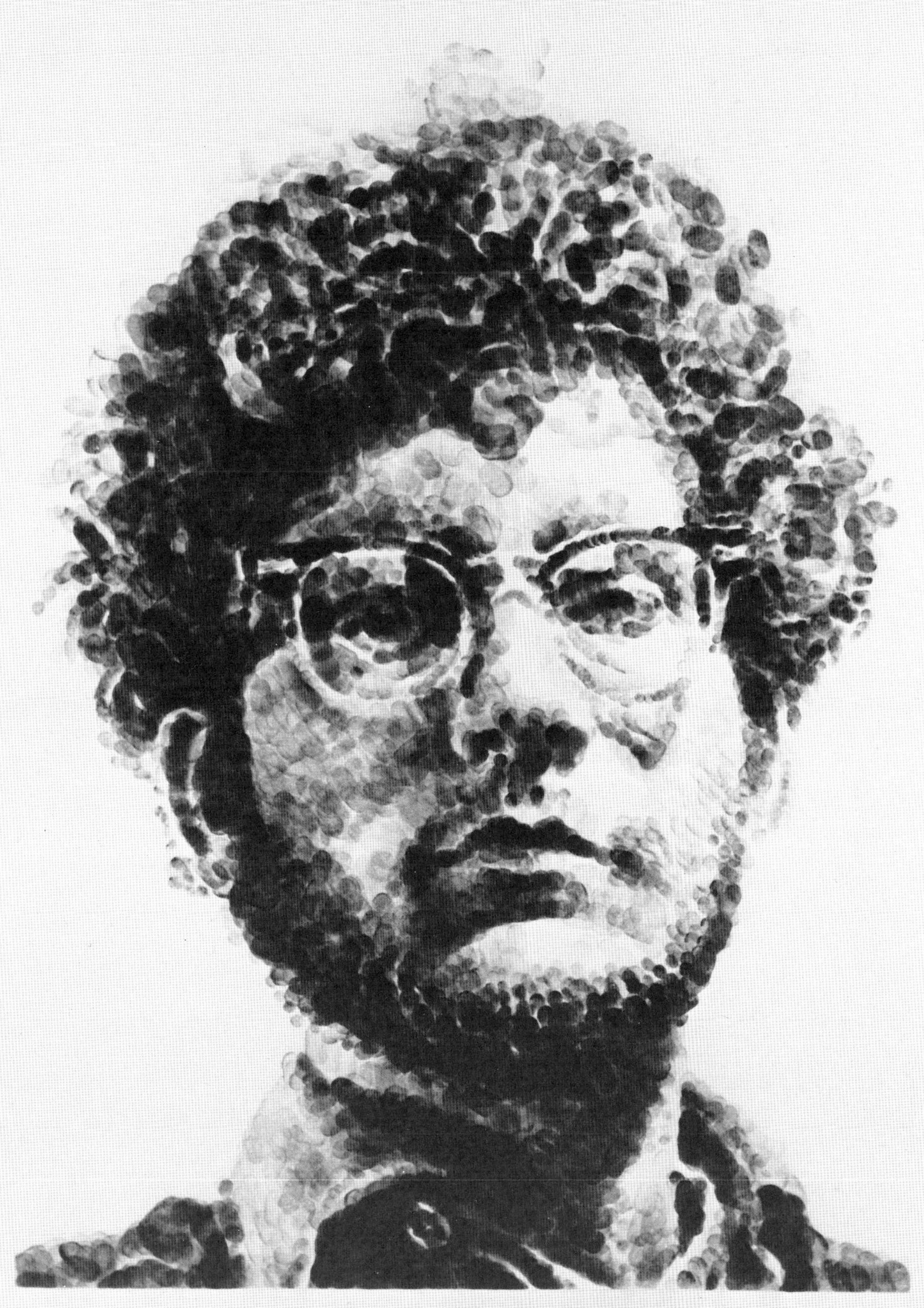

Bevan, 1981, fingerprint (litho-ink) on paper, 43 x 30¼″

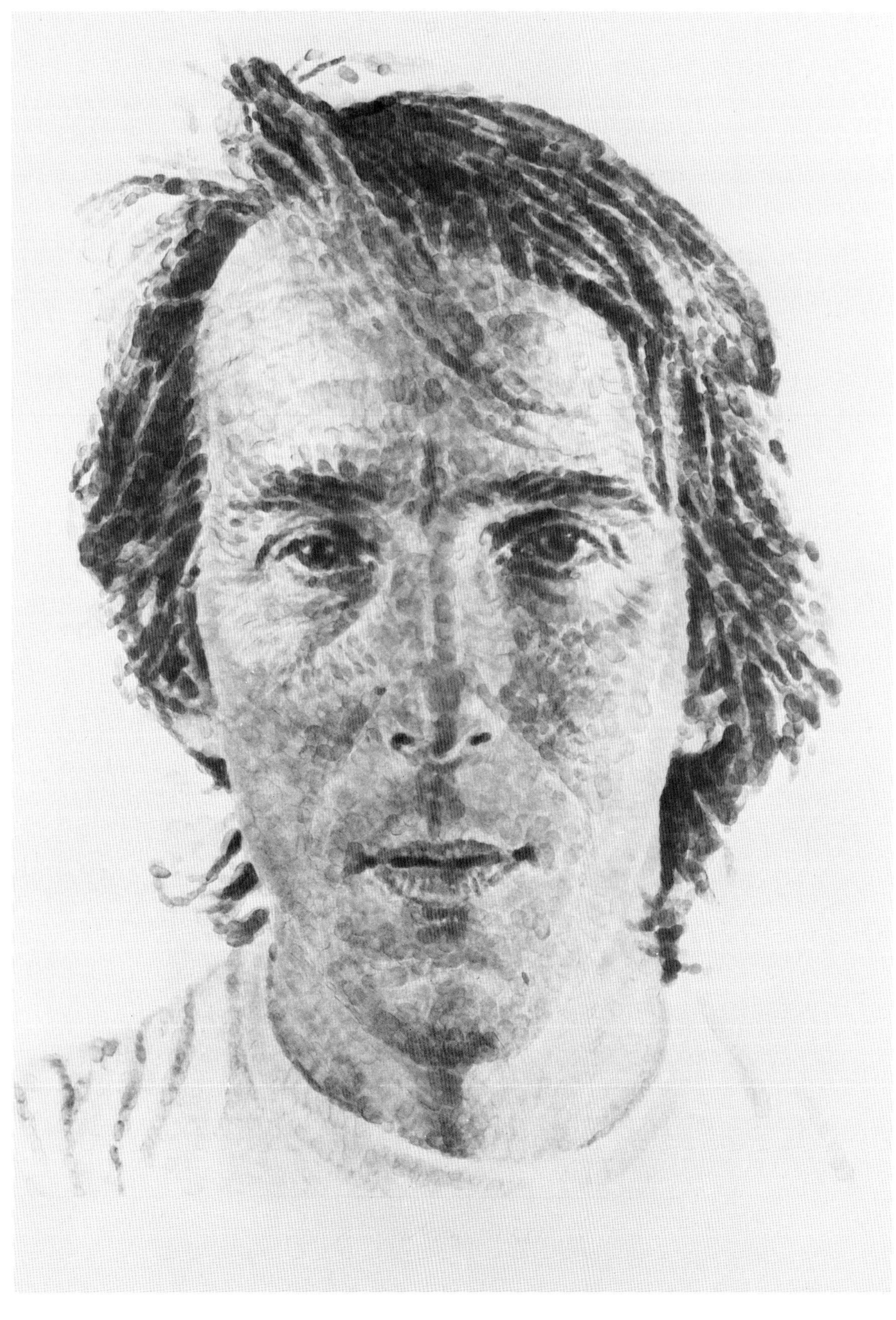

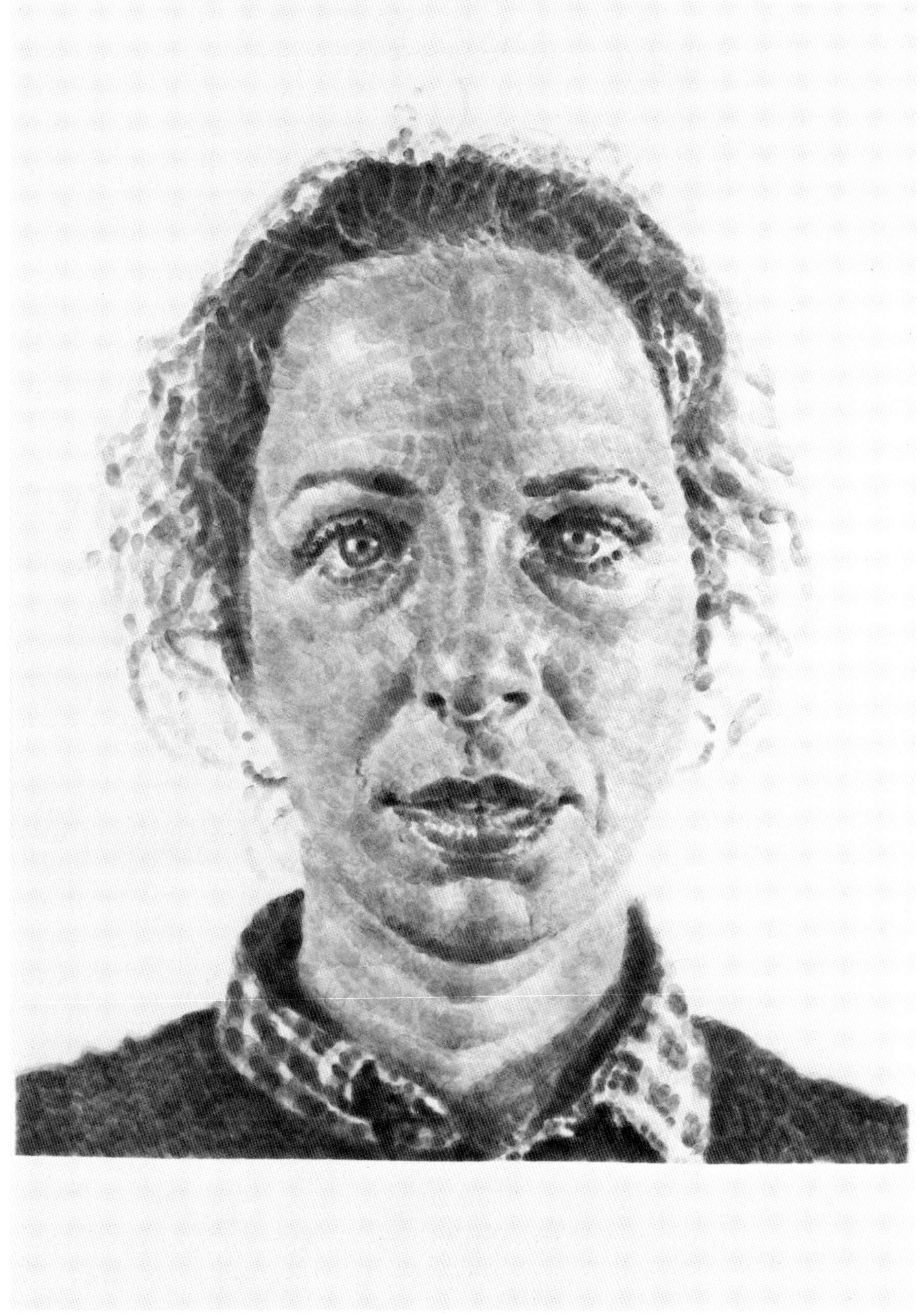

Leslie, 1981, fingerprint (stamp pad ink) on paper, 43 x 30½″

GWYNNE

Gwynne, 1981, fingerprint (stamp pad ink) on paper, 43¼ x 30¼"

Gwynne, 1981, fingerprint (stamp pad ink) on paper, 28¾ x 21½"

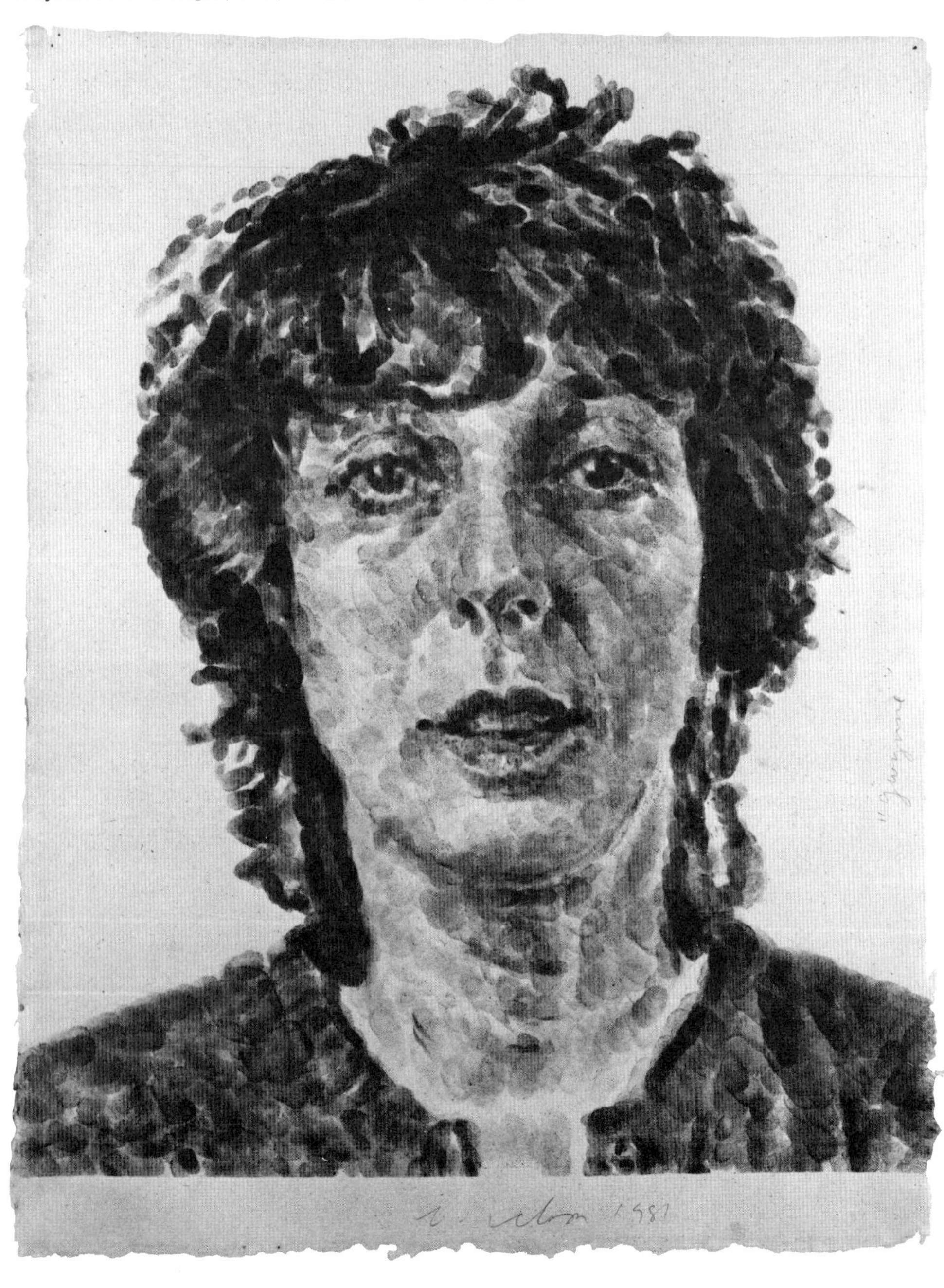

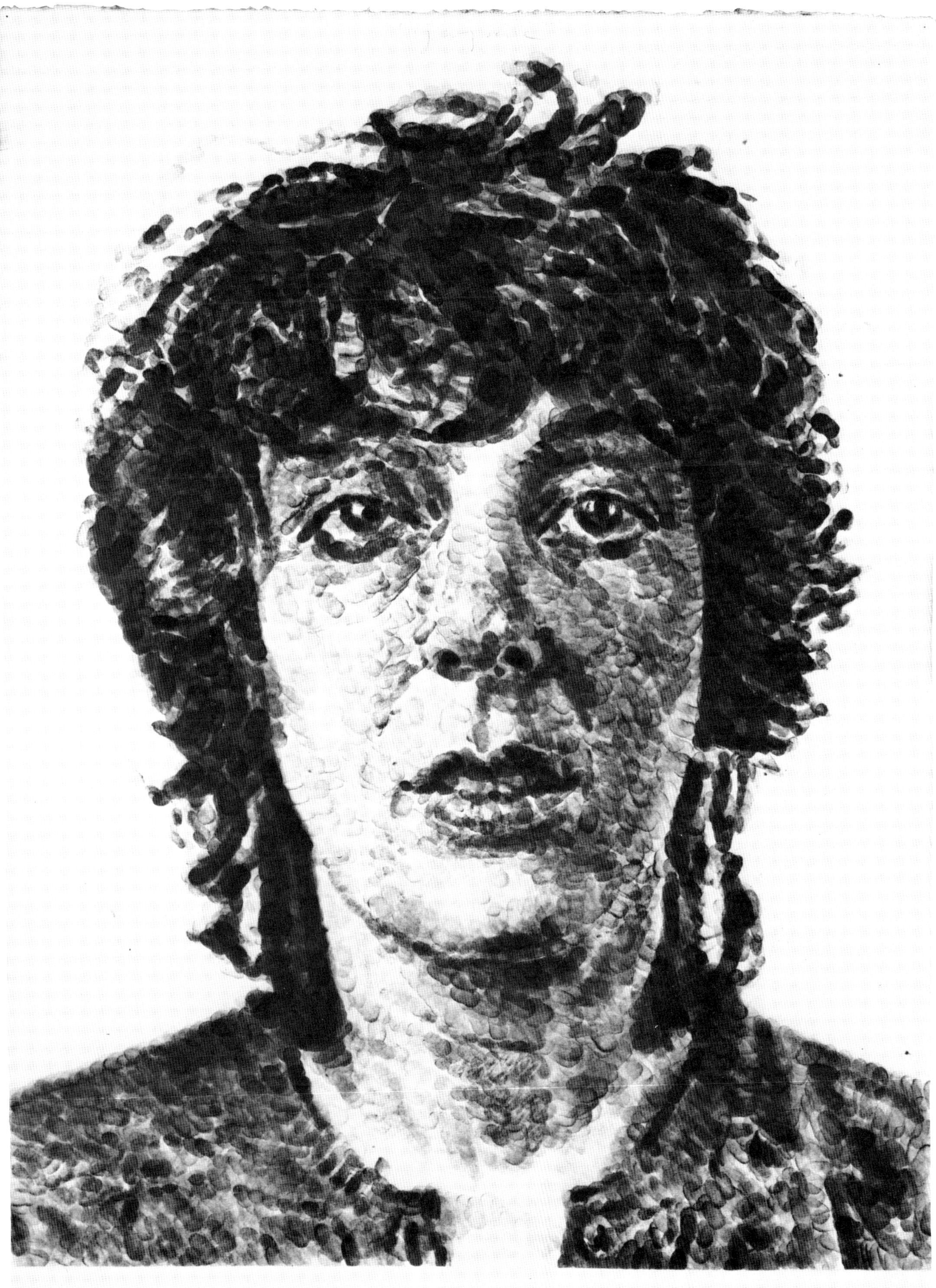

Gwynne, 1981, watercolor on paper, 29¾ x 22½″

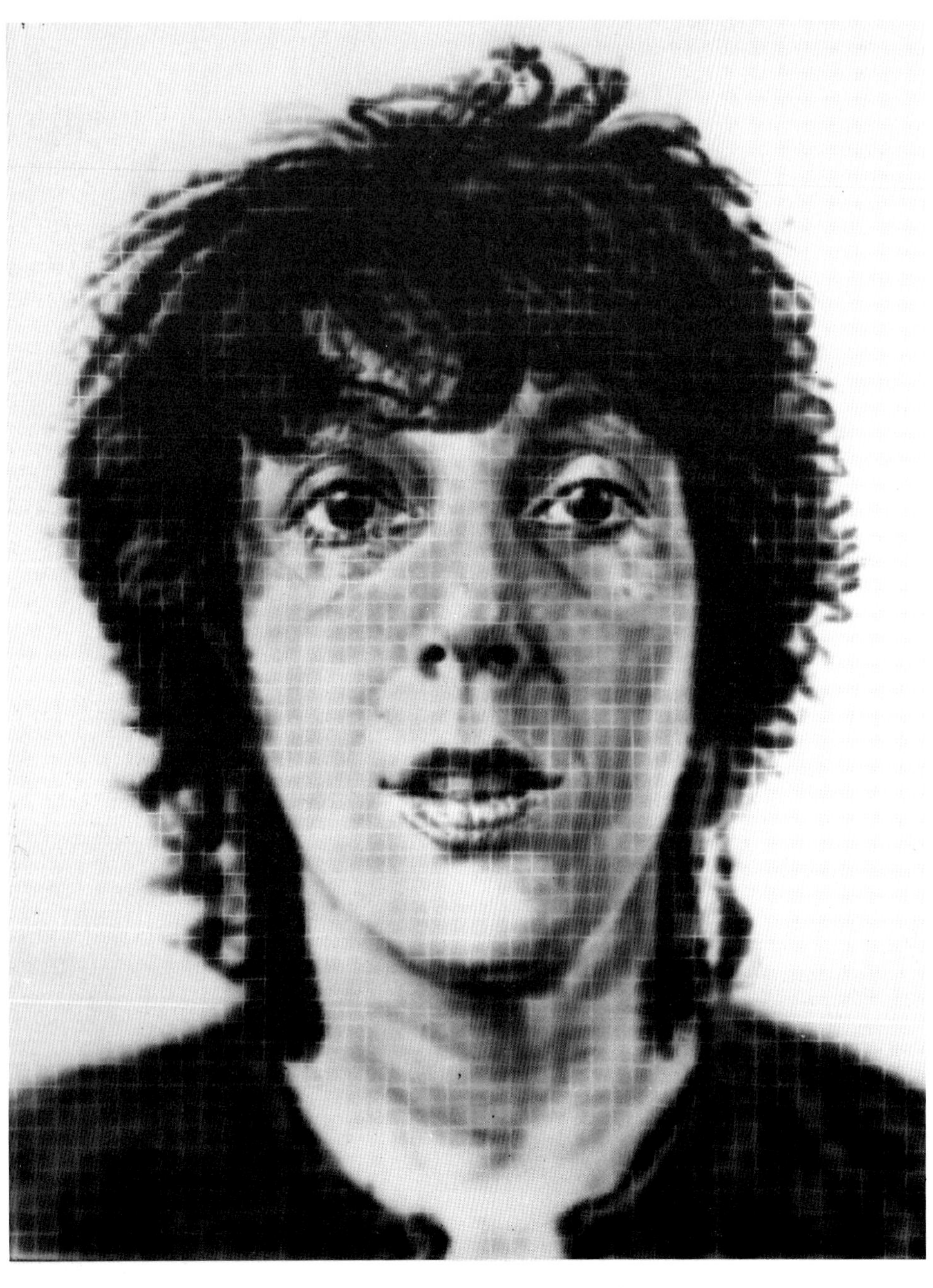

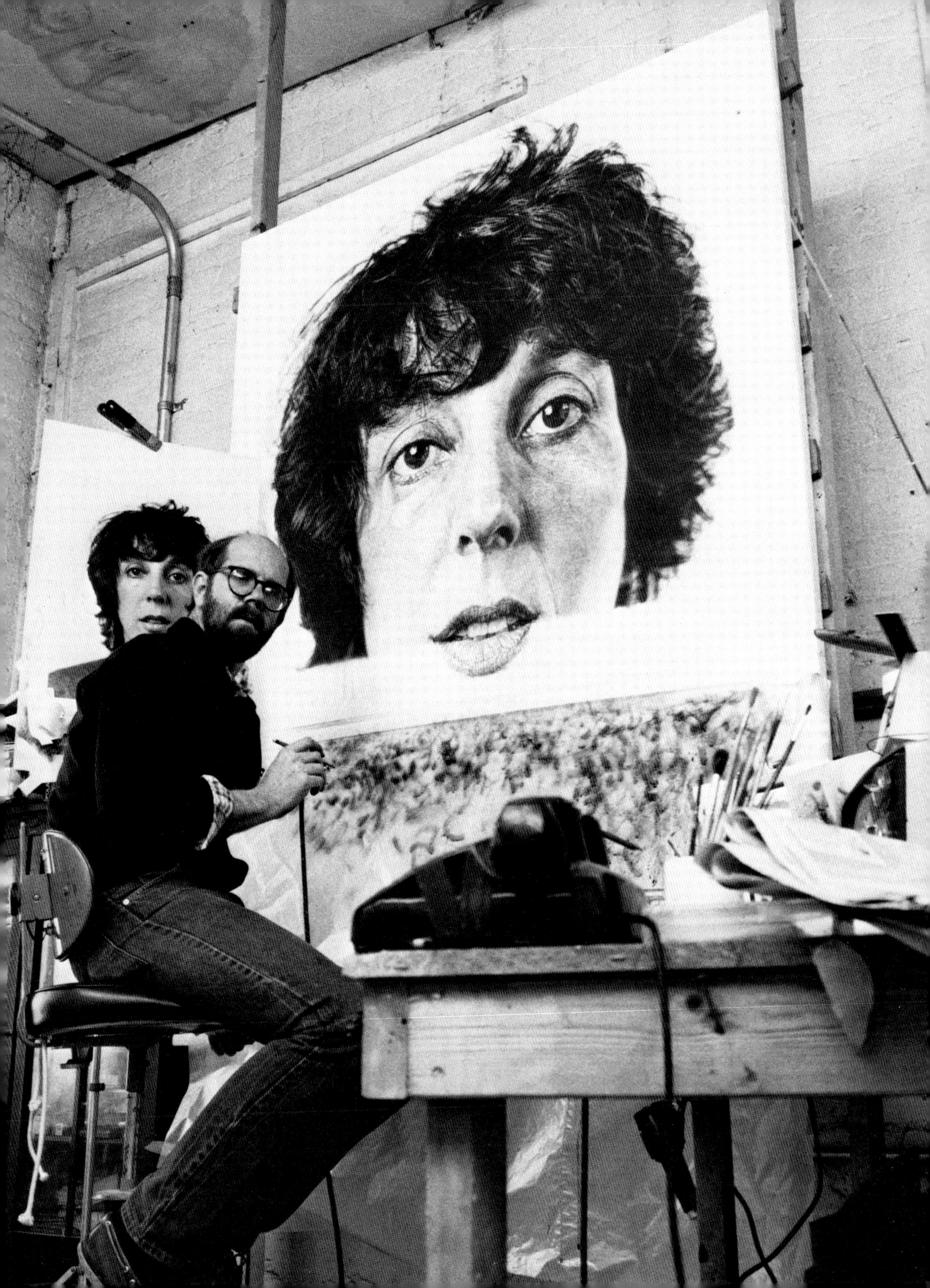

Gwynne, 1982, watercolor on paper mounted on canvas, 74¼ x 58¼″

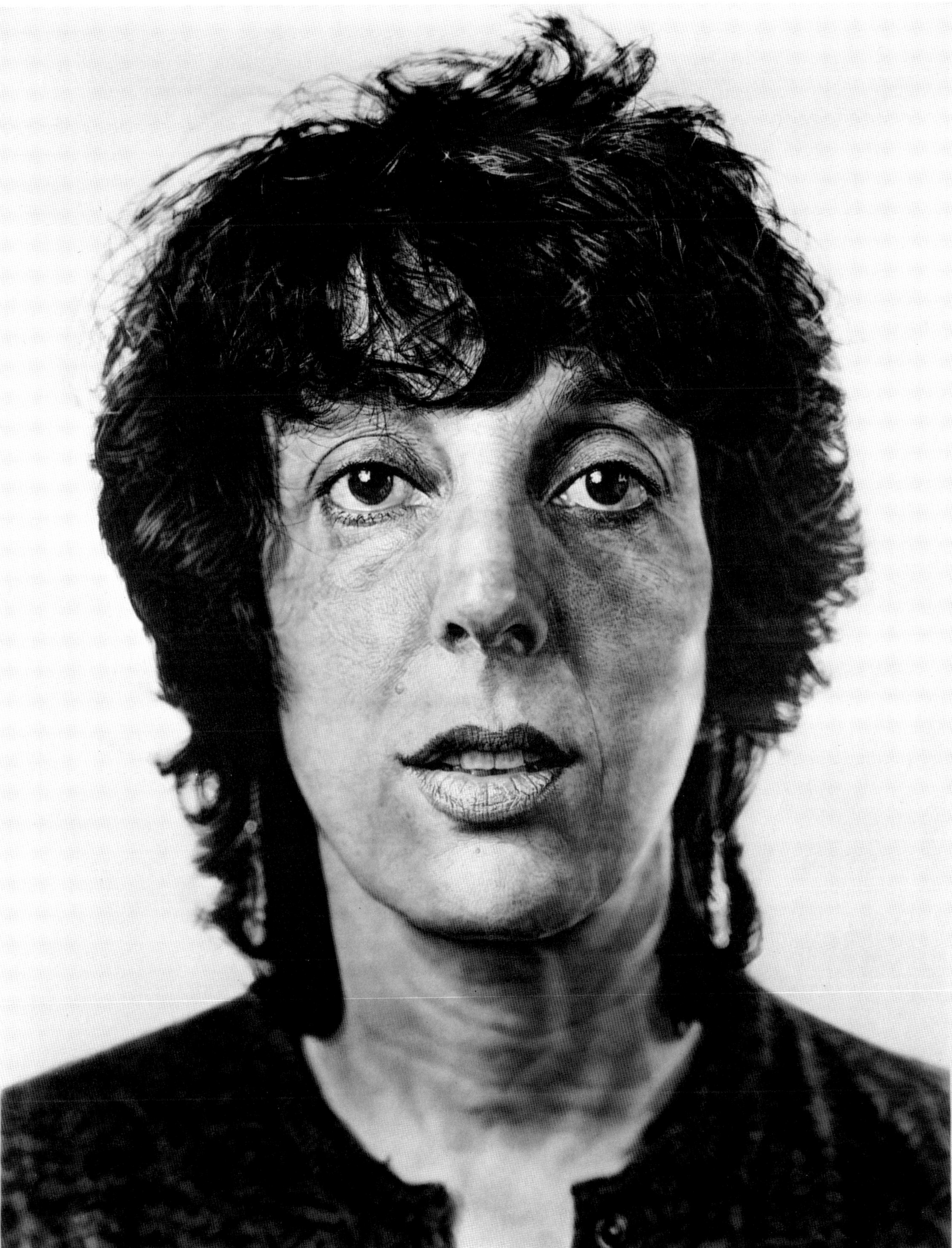

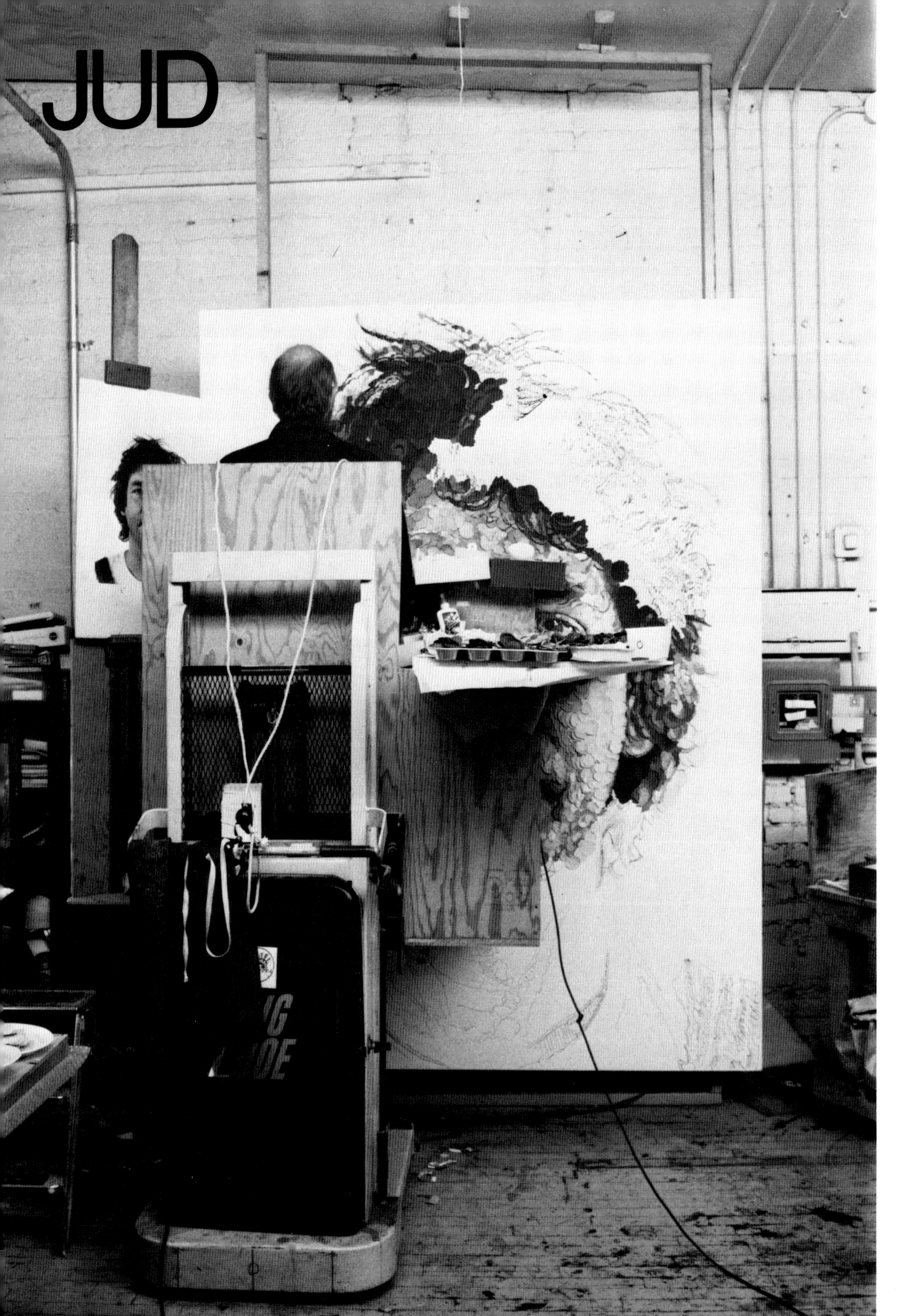
JUD

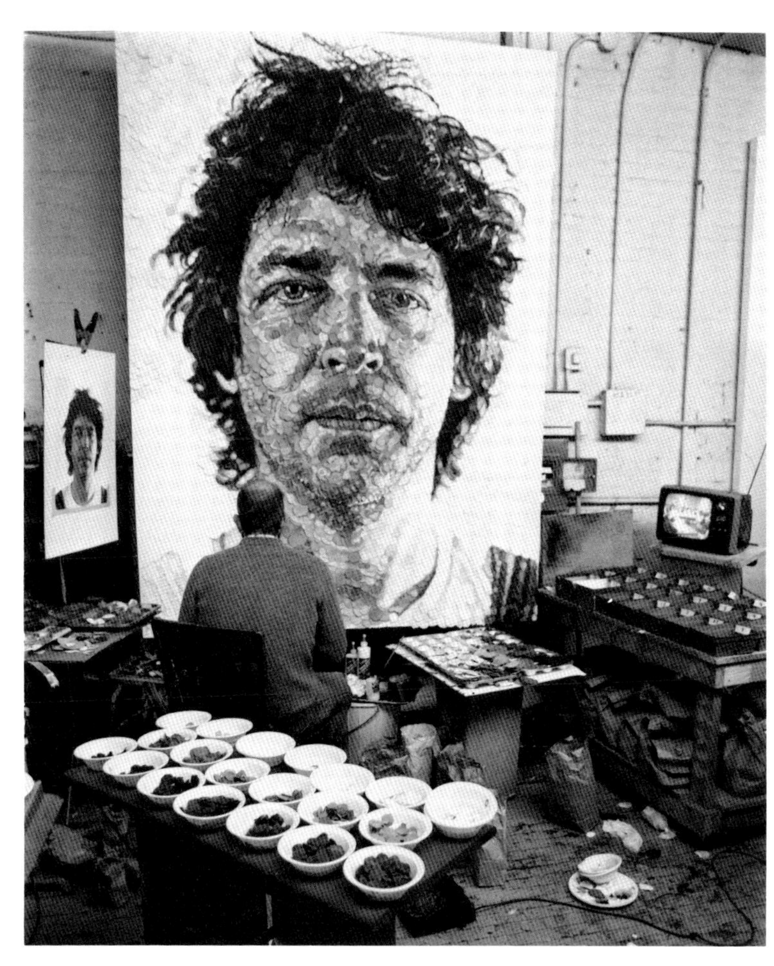

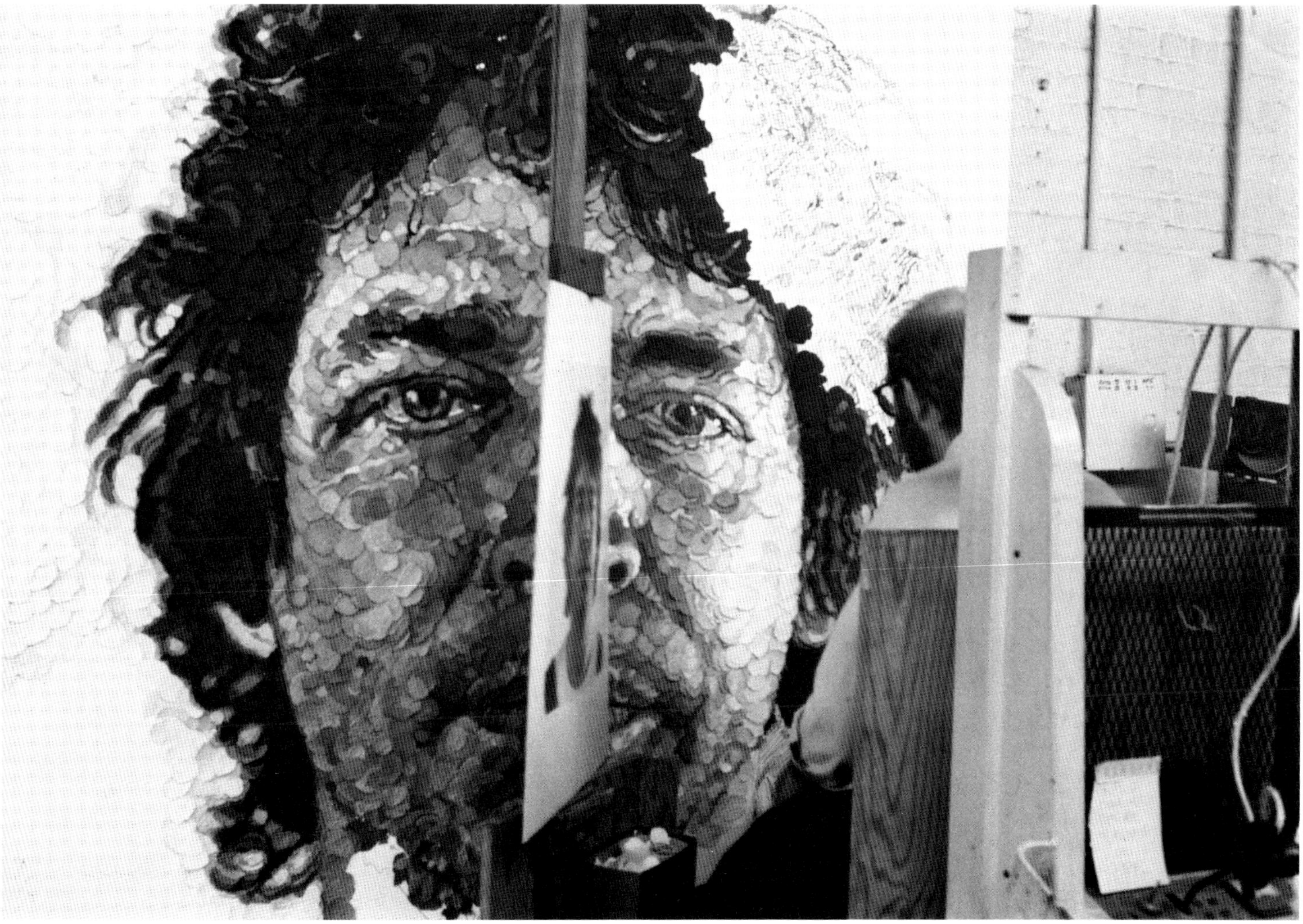

Jud, 1982, pulp paper collage on canvas, 96 x 72″

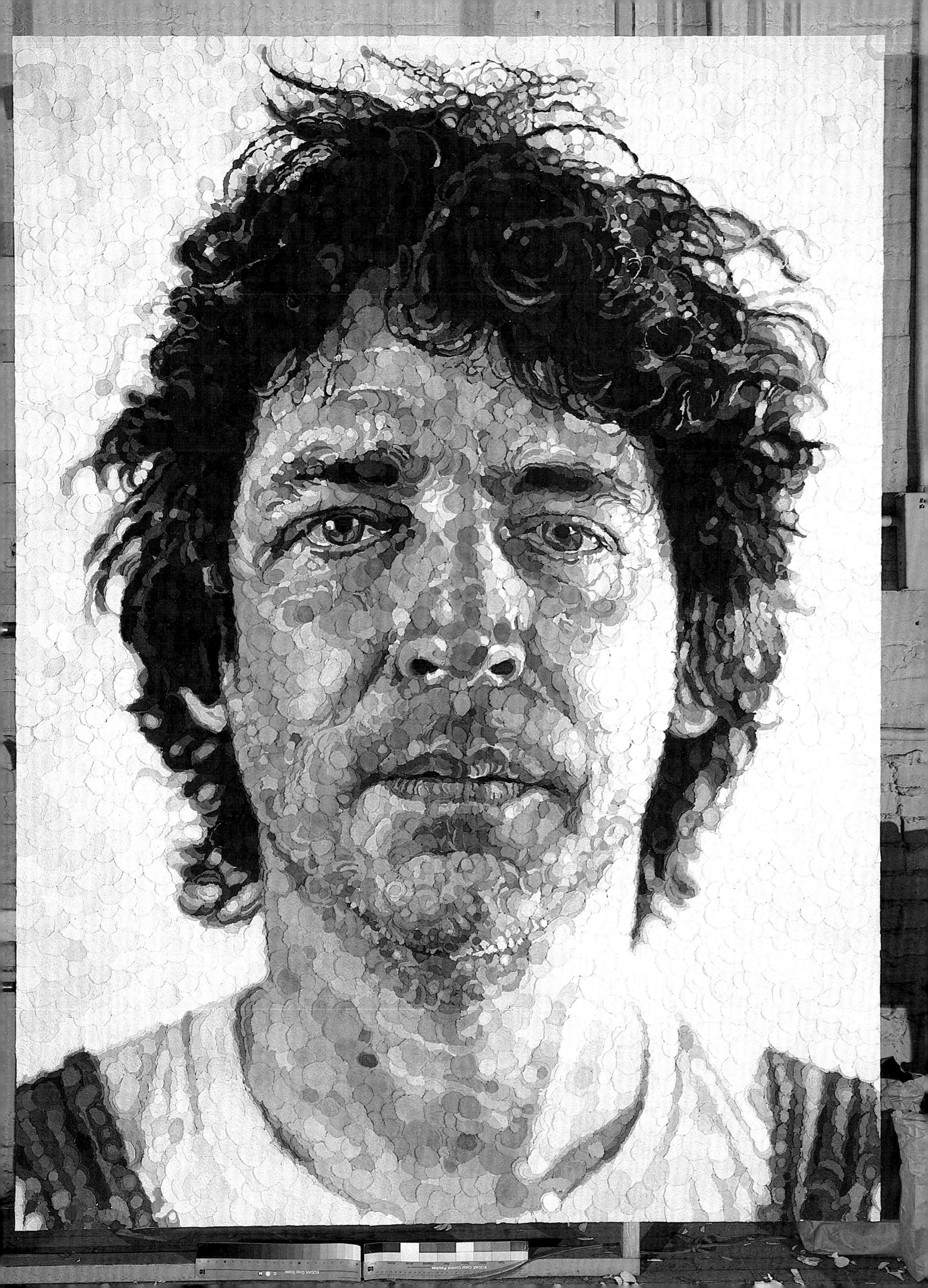

Leslie, 1982, pulp paper collage on canvas, 24 x 20″

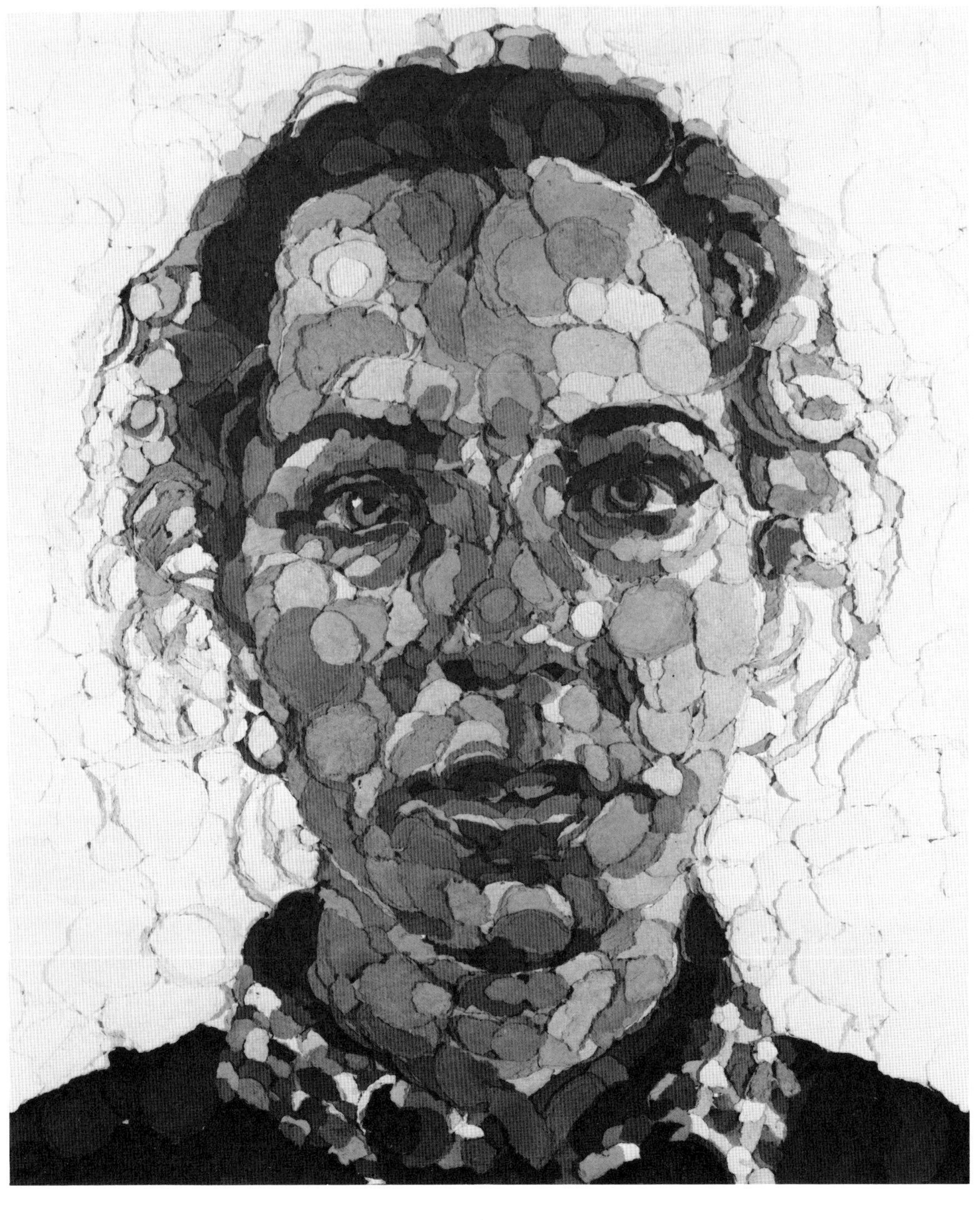

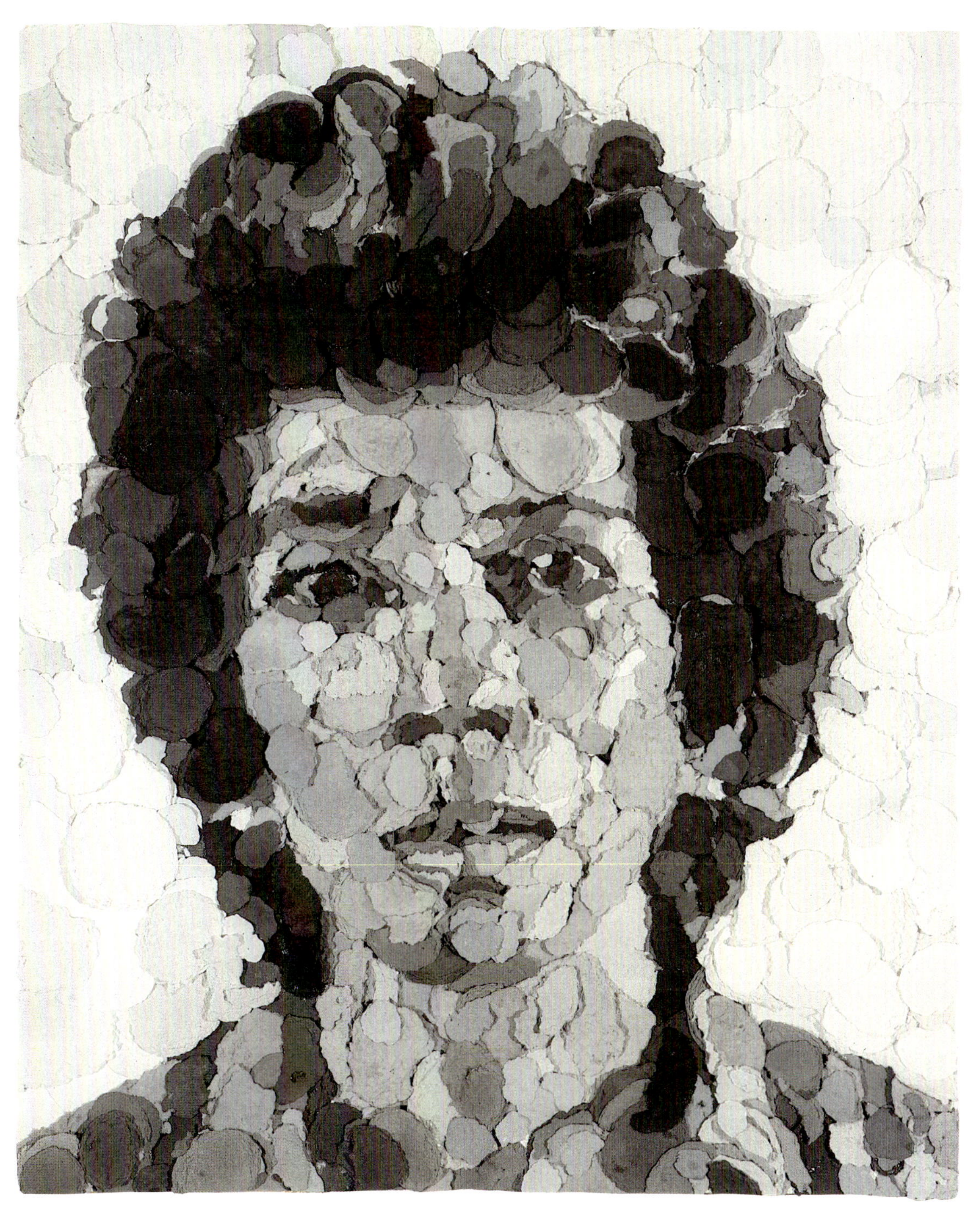

Phyllis, 1982, pulp paper collage on canvas, 24 x 20″

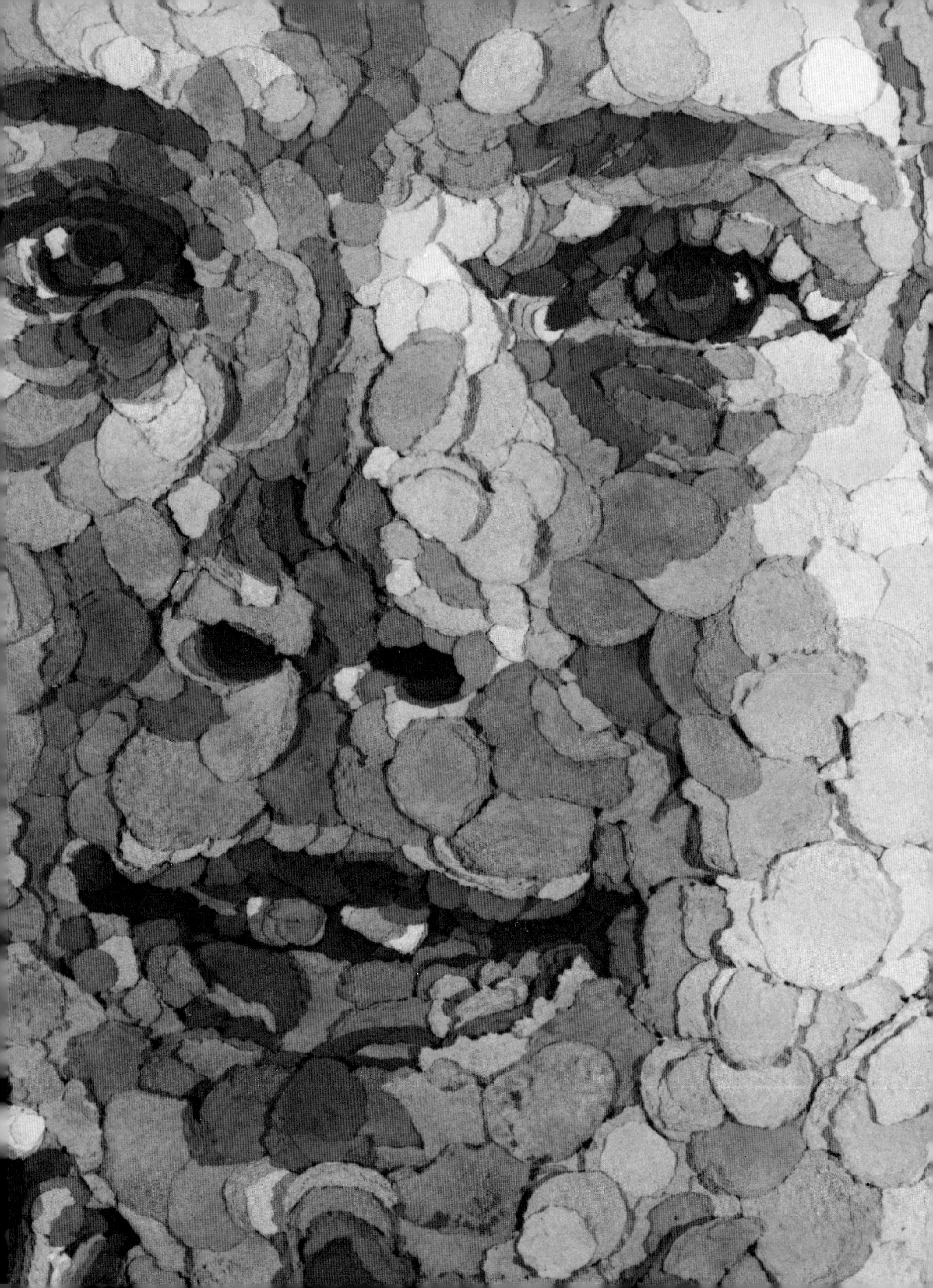

Georgia, 1982, pulp paper collage on canvas, 48 x 38″

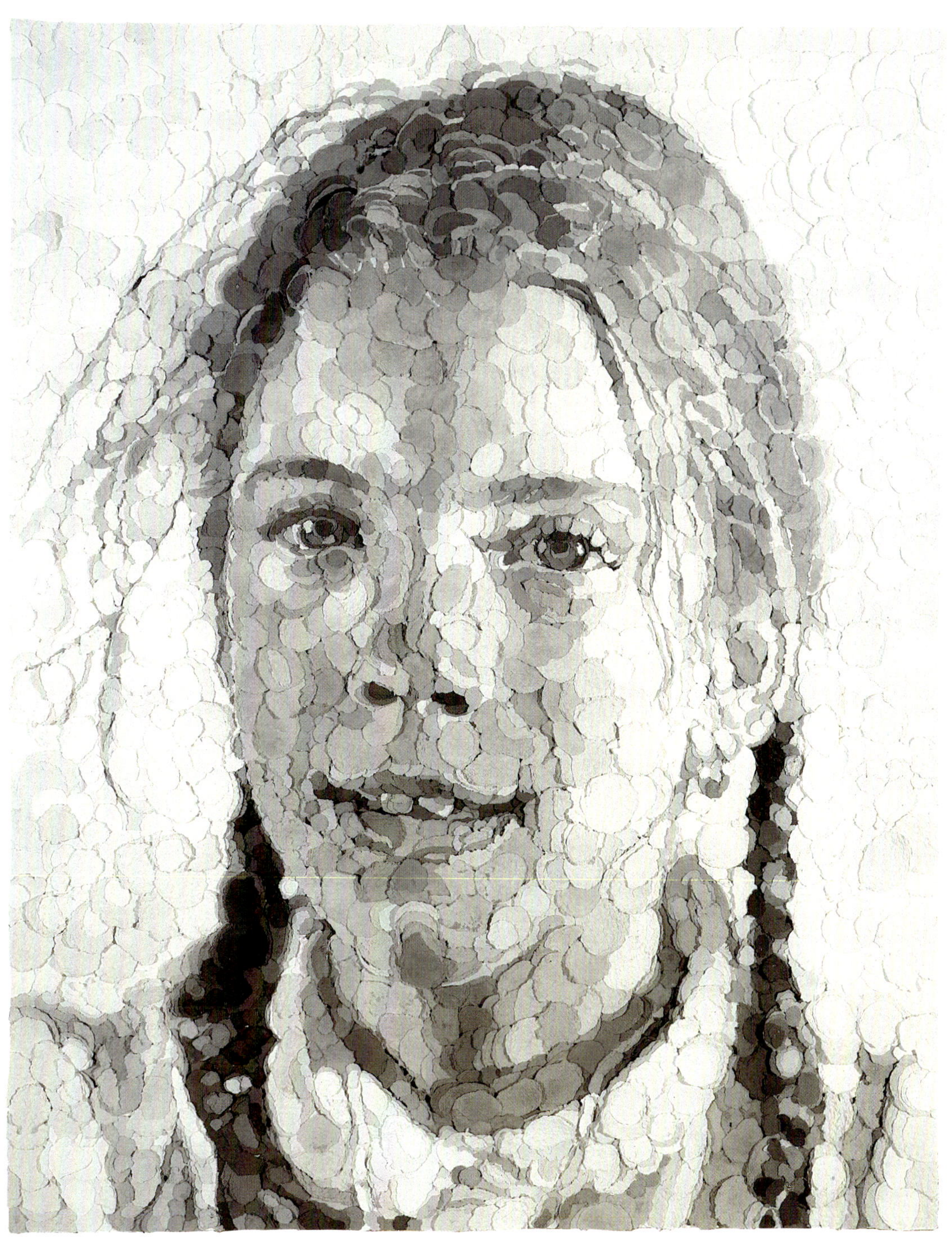

SOLO EXHIBITIONS

1967   Art Gallery, University of Massachusetts, Amherst

1970   Bykert Gallery, New York City

1971   Bykert Gallery, New York City
Los Angeles County Museum of Art, Los Angeles

1972   Museum of Contemporary Art, Chicago

1973   Akron Art Institute, Akron
Bykert Gallery, New York City
The Museum of Modern Art, Projects Gallery, New York City

1975   Art Museum of South Texas, Corpus Christi
Ball State University Art Gallery, Muncie
Bykert Gallery, New York City
Edwin Ulrich Museum, Wichita State University, Kansas
Laguna Gloria Art Museum, Austin
Minneapolis Institute of Art, Minneapolis
Mint Museum of Art, Charlotte
Phoenix Art Museum, Pheonix
Portland Center for Visual Arts, Portland
San Francisco Museum of Art, San Francisco
Texas Gallery, Houston

1976   Baltimore Museum of Art, Baltimore
Contemporary Art Center, Cincinnati

1977   The Pace Gallery, New York City

1977-78   Wadsworth Atheneum, Hartford

1979   Georges Pompidou Centre, Musee Nationale d'Art Moderne, Paris, France
Kunstraum Munchen, Munich, West Germany
The Pace Gallery, New York City

1980-81   Walker Art Center, Minneapolis, *Chuck Close 1968-1980*. Travels to
Saint Louis Art Museum, Museum of Contemporary Art, Chicago,
and Whitney Museum of American Art, New York

1983   The Pace Gallery, New York City